A Mod
Guide to Etiquette

Sarah Ivens is the Editor-in-Chief of *OK!* magazine in America. She has written for *Tatler, GQ, Cosmopolitan, Marie Claire, Men's Health, InStyle,* the *Daily Mail* and the *Mirror.* She is a born and bred Londoner who now lives in New York City.

Sarah's other books, *A Modern Girl's Guide to Getting Hitched, A Modern Girl's Guide to Networking, A Modern Girl's Guide to Dynamic Dating, A Modern Girl's Guide to Getting Organised, A Modern Girl's Guide to the Perfect Single Life* and *The Bride's Guide to Unique Weddings* are also published by Piatkus.

A Modern Girl's Guide to Etiquette

How to get it right in every situation

S A R A H   I V E N S

piatkus

PIATKUS

First published in Great Britain in 2003 by Piatkus Books Ltd
Reprinted 2003, 2004 (twice), 2005, 2006, 2010, 2011,
2012, 2013, 2014 (twice)

A CIP catalogue record for this book
is available from the British Library.

ISBN 978-0-7499-2424-9

Edited by Lizzie Hutchins
Illustrations by Megan Hess
Text design by Paul Saunders

Printed and bound in Great Britain by
Clays Ltd, St Ives plc

Papers used by Piatkus are from well-managed forests
and other responsible sources.

MIX
Paper from
responsible sources
FSC® C104740

Piatkus
An imprint of
Little, Brown Book Group
100 Victoria Embankment
London EC4Y 0DY

An Hachette UK Company
www.hachette.co.uk

www.piatkus.co.uk

Dedication

To my Grandma Mollie and Great Aunt Joan –
who taught me good manners cost nothing.

Contents

Contents

Introduction

I N THE MODERN AGE, knowing what to do, when to do it and even, sometimes, who to do it with, can be a pretty scary business. There's so much pressure to make the right impression, it's a wonder anyone ever steps outside their front door. No one likes to be thought of as rude, ill-mannered or ignorant. But help is at hand. With this book, I hope to make it a little easier for you to face every possible situation with grace, style and confidence. Trust me, there's no need to stay inside for the rest of your life.

We're only human, of course, and sometimes stress, tiredness or general lacklustre laziness takes hold. We all have off days when we become grumpy, selfish, rude, bored and intentionally irritating. If only we understood that a little effort with other people would make these dull periods pass so much quicker. In fact, it's been medically proven that paying someone else a genuine compliment or lending a helping hand can encourage even the most miserable, old swine to respond in kind. So there you have it: being friendly, polite and respectful will make you happy. 'Nuff said?

Well... almost. Treating others the way you would like to be treated is the first rule of etiquette, so being friendly, polite and respectful is an important base. But what do you do in new, confusing scenarios? How can you make strangers feel comfortable? And how can you defuse situations when others aren't as socially intelligent and caring as you are?

Over the next ten chapters, we'll be covering etiquette – but with a twist. The word 'etiquette' conjures worrying images of curtseying before royalty, carrying handkerchiefs and using the right cutlery – all useful and necessary lessons, I'm sure, but not as useful as learning when it is acceptable to use your mobile, how not to offend your new boss at an office party and how to tell your best friend her bum really does look too big in *that* dress. It's all about modern manners. That's the twist. A useful code to get you from A to B without getting punched.

I am no plum-voiced social butterfly, I'm an Eastender whose parents 'made good' and moved to Essex... and maybe that's why I am so interested in modern manners. When I went to university and started to mix with the upper classes, I realised that good behaviour has nothing to do with money, connections or where you grew up. Sure, it has everything to do with breeding – your parents teach you right and wrong, please and thank you – but being a decent person is not a class issue. It's about being kind.

When I told my parents I was writing about etiquette, my dad thought it was hysterical. 'What do you know? You wear trainers to work, dance on chairs and chew gum! And you're only 27 years old.' So does being young disqualify you from knowing right from wrong? Of course not! In fact, as the world changes, all our traditions and systems are questioned and radicalised, and we – the new generation – need to know the score as quickly as possible. We need a code of conduct for the modern age.

There's so much to say, so much to cover, but I've divided this book into ten important subjects and included vital rules, tips and real-life advice from people just like you – modern girls who want to get on with life while getting along with others. So let's begin and chink our glasses to many, many years of being cool, calm and collected.

Chapter One

Living standards

THERE ARE BASIC RULES for everyday manners that will make your life – and the lives of those around you – *so* much easier. Nothing's set in stone and I won't pretend that there is one foolproof way to behave in any situation. But if you start by doing to others as you would be done by, you won't go far wrong.

Minding your Ps and Qs

Keep it simple

It costs nothing to say 'please' and 'thank you'. This is a given. If anyone does anything for you – even if you didn't ask for it and you're not particularly grateful – thank them.

With 'please' and 'thank you', however, remember quality counts, not quantity. As long as they are meaningfully said, or implied, the number or exact wording is irrelevant.

Never say 'thank you' with attitude. People aren't stupid and sarcasm will undermine any gesture.

Sorry seems to be the hardest word...

But it doesn't have to be. When someone walks into you, treads on your foot, eats the last chocolate, etc., the word 'sorry' should be an 'easy come, easy go' commodity. If it makes life easier in everyday situations, you say sorry first. Even if something doesn't offend you, if someone in your company is visibly upset, apologise. Even if you think someone is a little too sensitive, that's their issue, so apologise. If you feel mutually responsible but want an easy life, make sure you're the bigger human and apologise first. This one little word is a big peacemaker and can stop resentment and bitterness firmly in their tracks. If you are too proud to take the blame for small things, practise. It's a great skill and doesn't mean you're weak. It means the exact opposite.

That being said, some people use the word all too easily – saying 'sorry' does not absolve you of responsibility or give you an automatic 'Get Out of Jail Free' card. It goes a long way, but should not be seen as a licence to do whatever you want.

Keep it clean

Oh f*** it, this is a difficult decision for any modern girl –
to swear or not to swear? Let's be honest, we all enjoy
cursing when angry, excited or just exclaiming displeasure.
However, the key phrase to keep in mind is 'there's a time
and a place'. Think before you speak and maybe even take
a quick look around. Swearing at the top of your voice on a
rollercoaster may seem like the most natural reaction in the
world, but check out the car behind you and consider the
worried mother covering her children's ears. There are
obvious rules for certain groups: in-laws, no way; mates at
work, oh yes! Unfortunately we usually learn the hard
way...

One thing does hold true, even for modern girls –
swearing is the last resort of expression. It's even worth
remembering that some pals, however close, won't be quite
so comfortably profane and can be offended, though
unwilling to point out their displeasure. Avoiding the exple-
tives and using more colourful, clever words to express
yourself will make you look intelligent, able and dignified –
especially in an argument. So be cool and opt for the child-
friendly words. And remember there is a distinct difference
between using swear words to emphasise a point and as a
direct insult. The latter is *never* ideal (though sometimes
inevitable).

Queue clues

I'm afraid there's no strategy that works well here other
than just do it. Queue. You'll get there quicker in the long
run... and with less fuss, stress and bother. It's polite
and fair.

Jo, 28

❝ I always get agitated by queue jumpers. At the check-in desk on a recent holiday a bloke decided to ignore the 20 people standing behind my family and came and stood next to us. Others then came and joined behind him, forming an entire second queue. Even though we had pre-booked seats, I still saw it as my goal to make sure that we got to the check-in desk before him, making comments in that "just meant to be heard" volume the whole way! ❞

If someone tries to push in, politely show them where the back of the queue is and give them the benefit of the doubt – unless they refuse to take their rightful place. If they refuse to budge, pity the ill-bred idiots (but quietly or you might get punched).

NB There is one queue you can jump. When you're really desperate and the line for the ladies' loo is a mile long, if the men don't mind, it is acceptable to dash into the gents'. Wait till the men have cleared out though, and if there's someone at the urinal when you make your exit, avert your eyes. And don't complain about the smell – men can be gross, but it was your choice to venture in there.

Gesticulating

Don't. Keep your hands to yourself. When not used ironically (for a cheap laugh with your mates) flipping the bird/ giving the one or two-finger salute/turning the volume up, etc., looks very, very crass. So does raising a fist or pretending to strangle someone. Save public hand-waving for cheerful hellos or politely getting someone's attention.

Two classic annoyances: pointing is one of the easiest ways to make someone feel intimidated and show your disrespect, as is talking behind your hand in a thinly veiled attempt to look discreet. You don't look discreet, you just look rude.

Meeting and greeting

Who would have thought saying 'hello' could be so tricky? When to kiss, when to hug when to shake hands...? One false move and you look like a Jezebel or a social stiff!

We all have our own ways of communicating with our friends and family, and what's right for one person may not be appropriate for another. But there are useful tips for handling other situations.

Colleagues

Just say 'Hello.' There's no need for physical contact until you've bonded at the Christmas party and are kissing each other good night. Then on Monday, go back to non-touching.

If you have a workmate you can't stand, it's always best to try to remain civil and in contact – rigorously 'blanking' someone in the office usually makes you look worse than them. And of course, you never know what someone might be dealing with in their personal life. Polite contact is always the safest option.

Bosses
Always stay as formal as possible until you know the territory. Let them lead the way and never assume that you can follow a colleague's behaviour.

New or distant family members
You're close in one way, but have no idea how to approach them? My advice is it's better to be friendly than formal. It's better to leave a meeting thinking you were excessive than mull over whether another person is thinking you were rude or is amazed by your standoffishness.

Shops/restaurants
Always make eye contact and always be polite. Just because someone is paid to serve you doesn't mean you can act superior. A 'hello' and a 'thank you' are essential.

Foreigners
If you are unsure of cultural practice, shake hands and be sure to smile a lot. If in doubt about what message you are conveying, a grin goes a long way. That is, until you get to know them, and then go along with the local trend, be it one, two or three kisses on alternate cheeks.

If you are meeting foreigners in a professional environment, do your homework beforehand – it's no good realising you've offended your prospective client on the plane home.

Boyfriends/husbands/lovers
In public keep your physical activities to a minimum – and yes, I know I sound like a prude, but no one, regardless of sexual orientation, should provide a live sex show on a street corner. It makes others feel embarrassed, lonely or – God forbid – perverted. Obviously, when it's dark and

you've had a bit too much too drink, having a snog while you're waiting for a train/taxi/parent to pick you up is more acceptable. You're trying to keep warm and conscious.

Children

This is a very tricky area. You should never insist that a relative/friend's child behaves in a certain way when greeting you. It's not your place to insist they stay silent, come over to say hello or, even worse, give you a kiss or hug. Leave it to the child or the parent to decide what's appropriate.

Kissing to be clever

Some people will always try and kiss you immediately – not because they like you, but because they are trying to look chic, network or are just a bit too touchy-feely. Don't be embarrassed if you stick out a hand as they turn their cheek. Greeting people like this is like playing scissor, paper, stone. You'll never know what they think is appropriate, but as long as you have made a positive gesture everything else will follow.

Air-kissing can look incredibly pretentious. If you don't like the person enough to touch skin, what are you doing pretend-kissing each other? I'm not asking you to elaborately suck their cheeks off instead, but the whole two-inch gap greeting looks ridiculous and merely serves to underline your emotional distance.

Post-kiss, a well-mannered thing to do is help a lady with a lipstick mark on her cheek. She'd rather a stranger told her than discover it herself at the end of the day. (The same applies to telling others about tucked-in skirts, sticky-out labels and the classic toilet-paper-on-shoe scenario. You will have ten seconds of mutual torment, but that's better than a day of regret.) Again, do unto others...

> **AMANDA**, 29
>
> ❝ I once got caught in a ten-second mini-Maori rugby stand-off with a business contact which seemed to last for minutes. I offered my hand. She went to kiss my cheek. So I jerked forward just as she went to shake my hand. Instead of getting my hand, she grabbed my now much nearer – and lowered – breast. It was too late to pull back and not kiss her by then, so I did – as she turned to apologise – and I ended up kissing her on the mouth. Cringe. I never saw her again. ❞

Confidence-boosters

Strangers will often mistake shyness for rudeness and someone lacking social confidence may appear sullen or indifferent. This is a serious problem – even movie stars are left crippled by it and many people turn to doctors and psychologists. Here are a few tips to make meeting new people easier:

◆ Make sure you are wearing clothes to make you feel comfortable/confident (depending on the situation).

◆ Focus on someone or something when you walk into a packed room. Don't let your eyes dart about nervously – you'll get dizzy.

◆ Don't worry about blushing – it looks charming and your hot cheeks will make people warm to you.

◆ Don't be ashamed to tell people you're shy. If they're kind, they will take you under their wing. If not, they're horrid, so ignore them.

◆ Smile, even when you don't feel like it.

◆ Work on your posture. Standing tall will instantly give you a boost.

◆ Imagine everyone naked (the old rules are the best) or that you've walked into a weird convention and they won't seem so scary.

◆ Don't drink heavily – it won't sedate your nerves and your view of the surroundings will be distorted.

◆ If you are standing with people and the host doesn't introduce you, do it yourself. Maybe the person-in-common has forgotten names. We've all done it.

Out and about

As soon as you step out of your front door, a plethora of mistakes awaits you... Here's how to cope.

Always on time

Punctuality is very important. Unless you want to get yourself a reputation for being inconsiderate and flaky, arriving when you say you will should be a priority.

There are always genuine reasons for keeping people waiting – weather, traffic, freak circumstances and illness can all put you behind – but 95 per cent of tardiness comes down to bad organisation. Be honest with yourselves, laydeez! It doesn't really take you 15 minutes to do your make-up for a big night out, does it? It's more like 30. And there you have it – already late!

There is an argument for being fashionably late, and yes, you can make an entrance at a party by arriving an hour after take-off. But it's rude to keep someone waiting on their own, in a restaurant and, especially, if a friend has offered to cook for you in their home. At least make a phone call to explain your whereabouts.

A mini on-time checklist:

1. Preparation. Make sure you have got money on you (last-minute trips to the bank take time).

2. Be realistic – if you have got a meeting at 5 p.m., don't arrange to meet your friends at 6 p.m.

3. Plan your route – allow double time during rush hour, etc.

4. If it's a toss-up between being hideously late when meeting friends or being on time but slightly dishevelled, your mates would rather see the natural 'you'. Groom in the loos later.

5. If you don't want to do something, say 'no'. If not, you'll resent going and drag yourself there resentfully, slowly… and late.

If you have an acquaintance who is always running behind, point out politely that you are busy and every half an hour is valuable, so if meetings need to be rearranged they should let you know.

When a friend is repeatedly arriving late, try the 'It's a shame you're late because we're going to have less time to catch up' line. If they continue to rebel against the conformity of Greenwich Mean Time, change the clock to suit them. Either say you're meeting earlier than you are or do what I do with a friend who is always late. It used to wind me up, but now if we've arranged to meet at 7 p.m., *I* get there for 8 p.m. I'm still often the first one there by a few minutes, but I'm not such a seething mass of anger.

Another way of dealing with latecomers is to point out the problem and get them to meet at locations that are easy for you – at a pub at the end of your road, in the reception of your workplace – and to call you on approach, or to join you on a night out with other, more reliable friends. In truly desperate times, steal the latecomer's watch and set it half an hour fast. They'll thank you one day.

Cleanliness is next to goddess-liness

OK, we all have busy schedules, but if there's one area of life in which it's unforgivable to cut corners it's personal hygiene. Smell is the most acute of the senses and a strange whiff can linger long in the memory. Fortunately these aren't medieval times, so there is no excuse for bad breath or body odour when presenting yourself to the world.

At all times keep a grooming kit in your bag or desk drawer containing deodorant, tweezers, a nail file, a packet of mints, spare underwear, ear buds, a mirror and a toothbrush. It may sound prissy, but it will stop you putting anyone off their dinner.

If you have a medical condition which is causing you social embarrassment, go to the doctor. It may be that your condition can be easily dealt with. And don't be worried, they really have seen it all before and won't judge you – unlike the poor commuter stuck next to you on a crowded train.

If you're paranoid about unnecessary or unwholesome distractions such as ear wax, rogue spots, stray hairs and dandruff, carry a mirror with you. Making the right impression is unfortunately as much to do with aesthetics as charisma. But put it this way, you're making sure that your good manners aren't undermined by anything trivial.

Scent test: do this before going out – even without a mirror!

1. Check your armpits for sweat patches, smells and deodorant marks.

2. Cup your hand and breathe into it to sniff your breath.

3. Ask a close – and trusted – mate/colleague to give you the once-over.

4. Lift up soles of shoes to check for dog's mess, chewing gum, etc.

A word about point 3 and telling someone a difficult hygiene truth: if you have a friend or colleague that you think might benefit from a gentle nudge about the merits of deodorant or similar, as long as you tread very carefully they will usually be grateful. Tips for doing this:

1. Always speak in private.

2. Decide early on whether to be direct or subtle. This will depend on your relationship.

3. If direct, come straight out with it. Be honest but gentle.

4. If subtle, try recommending an amazing new product that you've found. Even say you've 'bought one, got one free' and hand it over.

Public nuisance

The consumption of fizzy drinks and Irritable Bowel Syndrome are both on the rise, but it's still important to keep gas leakages under control. It is never acceptable to fart or burp in public. Remember there's rarely such a thing as a 'safe fart'. You will invariably fog out your neighbours or imitate a trumpet. Save it for the bathroom or a people-free farmyard.

In a similar vein, never comment on someone else's misfortune, especially if in an embarrassing location – you'll only make their misery worse. Of course you may end up being silently accused, but it's the only polite thing to do.

At the opposite extreme, remember you wear perfume to add gentle fragrance to your life, not to choke anyone unfortunate enough to be in the same room as you. Two squirts for day and three for night should suffice.

Along the lines of not polluting your environment, don't drop litter – find a bin or take it home with you. And smoking isn't acceptable everywhere, especially around the sick, pregnant or young. Always ask if those around you mind when you light up.

If you're not normally a smoker but occasionally fancy a cigarette, try not to always blag them off the same person. If you think you might partake, make an effort to buy a packet yourself, or give some cash to the person buying the fags. Never blow smoke in someone's face, even if they're smoking as well.

Sounding off

Any strange noises come as a surprise to those around you. Blowing raspberries, for example, evokes the obvious – not the thing for a modern girl. Making animal noises makes you sound like, well, an animal. And anything that strays too far from the yippee/whoop/aah/ouch/brrrr path will leave people thinking you're a bit doolally. Shush!

Keeping your cool

At times even the most laid-back, thoughtful soul can be tested. Fates seem to be conspiring against you or, worse still, people are acting like idiots. When faced with a difficult situation, don't turn a crisis into a drama – act with decorum. Here's how:

1. Breathe. Calm down and know that you can overcome anything. This is just a test of your brains, initiative and common sense. Look on it as a social workout.

2. Remember however hard things are now, they *will* get better. There is light at the end of the tunnel.

3. Don't look to blame others. That won't get you out of the muddle any quicker and could lead to false accusations and fall-outs.

4. You're not Wonder Woman. Do what you can then pass the buck or get others to help. The weight of the world doesn't have to rest on your shoulders.

5. Be decisive. Pick a route and go with it. Dithering gets you nowhere.

Call the fashion police!

Sadly, in our shallow world, what you look like counts for a lot. First impressions are generally made on appearance. But remember, style isn't about being a skinny giraffe, it's about being comfortable and confident.

Fashion without offence

1. Be honest with yourself. If you've gone up a dress size, buy up a dress size. You can always cut the labels out if you don't really want to admit it to yourself or others. There's no surer way to highlight the fact you're a little heftier than by squeezing your expanding rump into the same clothes.

2. Flashing your knickers? If you're wearing low-cut trousers, go for low-cut pants. If you think passers-by may still get an eyeful, make sure they're clean and pretty – perhaps even go for a colourful, sparkly pair for extra pizzazz. If you're wearing tight trousers, always go for a well-fitting G-string (if it's too tight, it will cut your hips in two, which has just as bad an effect as big granny bloomers).

3. Flashing your, er, stains? If something has a stain, smear or is dodgily creased, put it in the laundry basket. And don't be tempted to get it out again on a lazy morning.

4. Flashing your bits? Don't do this indiscriminately. All modern girls should learn when and how to show off their best characteristics. Keep cleavage and fanny pelmets under wraps while the sun is still shining or your family is visiting.

5. Beware of heel hindrances. Don't wear shoes that will have you limping, moaning or flagging behind your friends bent double. That's *so* not a good look. Pick heels to flatter your feet/height/outfit. Don't wear three-inch stilettos for the sake of it.

You wear it well – now sit up and listen

There's no point looking ladylike if you sit like a trucker with swollen balls. How you sit will turn the scruffiest pair of jeans into acceptable high-fashion daywear. The old-style sitting position for laydeez (legs crossed neatly) has now been dismissed as an instigator of varicose veins and circulation issues, so go for the simple legs together, slanted and tucked away. When I'm wearing trousers, I sometimes forget about the importance of this and sit around with my legs out and about… and then I'm always tripping people up or get photos back and realise my thighs look twice as mighty as the rest of me. Not a good look.

> **NB Do not go for hippy-groovy yoga** positions in any location that's not your gym or bedroom. People will think you're a loon and not concentrate on what you're saying.

Posture problems

Stand up straight: not only will you look taller and slimmer but your boobs will perk up a bit, your bum will tuck in and you'll look more confident. Everyone's a winner!

If often helps to imagine your stomach and back as an immovable core stabiliser which supports everything else. Practise walking with a book on your head if you must, or imagine you are being pulled towards the ceiling with invisible shoulder straps. Another tip is to walk with your stomach sucked in (this also helps big-belly days). Slouchers can get serious back problems, so it's not just a vanity issue.

If you can't focus on standing up straight, invest in a well-fitting bodice to force you into shape and make sure you're sleeping on a good mattress. Stretching exercises such as Pilates and t'ai chi can also work wonders.

Naked ambition

The only thing worse than wearing bad clothes is wearing no clothes. For example, topless sunbathing can make holiday companions feel inadequate or uncomfortable, so check first before whipping off your top. And find out what the local customs regarding this matter are.

Even wearing transparent items to an evening bash can render conversation impossible, as your acquaintance attempts to divert their eyes from your nipples to the buffet. Do the lighting test before you go out – check your all-round view in front of a bright light and in daylight. C-list celebs that show up to premières in little more than a lace veil and a piece of string always plead ignorance as to their see-through, tabloid-pleasing dress. Don't be as stupid (or trashy) as them.

If you want to flash more than you stash, make sure extra rolls of fat, cellulite and hairy bits are tucked away neatly. We're all women and we should all love our bodies whatever the shape or size, but others could be trying to eat. If you want to wear a thigh-skimming skirt on a windy day, wear sensible knickers. Likewise if you plan on bending over a lot.

Embarrassing situations

There are a few everyday places that always cause a little bit of unrest, but we should keep going to them, so what do we do? We cope. Here's how…

The gym

I've never understood women who actually enjoy sweating in Lycra whilst jumping up and down on a conveyor belt. Especially the skinny ones. But gyms are necessary evils in today's sedentary society, so how to get healthy with minimum stress?

♦ If you don't like the idea of communal changing-rooms and showers, get kitted up beforehand and shower at home.

♦ Buy yourself new workout clothes you feel happy and stylish in – too many women feel frumpy at the gym and it's not surprising when they're wearing a baggy T-shirt and their boyfriend's trackies.

♦ Work to your own pace (ask the trainer to sort you out a personal programme) and don't try and compete with those around you.

♦ When swimming, stick to the right side and speed for your lane.

♦ Always wipe a keep-fit mat after use.

♦ Persuade a friend to go with you to make it a social thang.

The doctor's surgery

Here, alongside the fear of being kept waiting for ages and picking up lots of nasty viruses, there's always the worry the doctor will think you're timewasting... Well, are you? No, so don't feel guilty about being there. And don't feel bad about moving away from the spluttering sneezers – you're right to be nervous. Ask to see a female doctor if it makes you feel more comfortable. Always wear underwear you're not worried about being seen in, in case you're asked to strip or lift your top up. And do purlease know that doctors are there to help and have seen *everything* a million times before. It's better to be safe than sorry.

Transport

Being shoved on a bus or train like cattle is not very dignified, especially in the rush hour when everyone's sweaty and rattled. Keep calm, take minimal luggage so you're not tripping people up and wear a good deodorant. If you've got a cold, remember tissues – everyone knows the awful sniffing that makes you self-conscious. Don't worry too much if you have a coughing fit: cover your mouth and know that everyone else has been there and should be feeling for you.

Forgotten to buy a ticket? Honesty is the best policy. Go to a guard. Even if he charges you a penalty fare, you'll have the moral upper hand.

Feel guilty for having a seat when others are standing? Always offer the space to the elderly, pregnant or disabled. If there aren't any worthy cases around, enjoy your good luck.

Finally as a modern girl you shouldn't get affronted if a bloke the same age/health is sitting down while you're standing. Chivalry is a great thing, but in life we can't expect to have our cake and eat it. Well, not all the time...

LALLA, 30

❝ I think it's important to say 'please', 'thank you', 'how are you?', and never push in. If you say you're going to do something for a mate – even if it's just calling them – then you should do it, otherwise, people just stop believing you. It's boring, but I treat people how I like to be treated – and am very old-fashioned in the sense that I always offer my seat on a tube to an elderly person, pregnant lady, etc, which should be the form. I am horrified people don't anymore. The thing that gets right up my nose is people who eat on trains and whilst they are walking around – especially that fast-food crap. It stinks, it's unpleasant to watch and usually the people munching are not very aesthetically pleasing... That sounds terrible, doesn't it? Generally, people are just less decent nowadays – they're pushy, aggressive and they don't care about anyone else's welfare. ❞

The spa

It can be intimidating stripping to your birthday suit, jumping up onto a table and offering your wobbly flesh to a professional. But they've seen it all before – and much worse – so don't be nervous. Most aren't that busy looking anyway, they focus elsewhere. A good therapist will explain what is about to happen and what items of clothing to leave on. If they don't, ask. You are allowed to. A few more tips:

◆ Don't worry if you forgot to put on matching underwear – you're having a treatment, not modelling lingerie. For a body treatment, you should be offered disposable paper knickers to wear anyway.

- Don't feel you have to make small talk. It's a compliment to the therapist if you relax . .. and even drift off.

- You don't have to tip for health and beauty treatments, but if it was great, ten per cent is a good guide.

- Keep your clothes on unless specified, i.e. in the sauna or steam room. Use your good judgement to suss out any pervs and don't feel bad about complaining if you find someone staring at you strangely through the mist.

- If you must use a sunbed, spray and wipe after use and don't faff around too long in there – there could be a queue forming outside.

HOLLIE, 28

❝ I had a horrific incident with an Israeli masseur about five years ago. To start with, it was a man! I couldn't believe it. He told me to strip and get on the bed while he was out of the room. I ignored the paper knickers (I didn't know what they were) and didn't know I was supposed to cover my modesty with the towel he'd left on the bed for me. So I just lay there with all my bits out and he didn't say anything, just kneaded me for half an hour. I found the experience far too sexual because my boobs were wobbling about all over the place, and I hated every minute of it. Now I know about the towel! ❞

Reunions

OK, so these aren't everyday occurrences but when you get invited to one, you know about it. Seeing people you've avoided for years brings up lots of questions – and nagging doubts that you've got fat/boring/wrinkly. But you should go. Blasts from the past can make you feel nostalgic and warm and updating – and editing – your new life to tell virtual strangers is a good opportunity for a bit of self-analysis. Everyone will be nervous, so admit that when you see the first friendly face and you'll be fine.

Shop changing-rooms

Check out which stores have communal trying-on areas and if you can't bear it, either buy before you try (keep all the labels on until you know it's perfect in case you need to return it) or go at a time you know the changing-room will be relatively empty.

Remember, all shops produce different sizes, so don't get upset if you're normally a size 12 and today you're a 14 – just buy what looks best and cut out the label.

Don't be put off by overbearing sales staff and don't let them push you into buying things. Just politely tell them you're fine and can look after yourself. If you need advice, take it from the well-dressed woman in the next cubicle, not the pushy salesperson.

On the road

There is a view that women make the better drivers, but we can still get road rage. As with all areas of life, consideration, care and calm will see you through your journey. Don't be a motor mouth when you get behind the wheel. Driving sensibly and respectfully is not only a matter of manners, it's a matter of life and death.

> **NB If you're a non-car owner**, don't ask to borrow a friend's car. Not only does it throw up insurance questions, but it's asking for trouble. For example, if you damaged the car, it would inconvenience your friend considerably while it was being fixed. If your mate doesn't mind lending you the car, they'll offer.

If you're a non-driver, don't take advantage of those who are. Always offer petrol money, offer to book a cab once in a while when you go out drinking so they can have a few sherbets, and if you have accepted a lift, leave when the driver wishes to leave.

Secrets of Success

◆ A little goes a long way. A smile costs nothing.

◆ Not everyone will like you, so don't worry about pleasing all the people all the time. Just act in a way that makes you proud. A toast that makes a lot of sense is 'Here's to those who wish us well, those who don't can go to hell!' Don't waste time on those who don't have your best interests at heart.

◆ Once you've been introduced to someone, acknowledge them whenever you meet. Even if you can't quite place them, say 'hello'. If someone you've met before doesn't respond to your greeting, take the moral high ground and move on.

◆ If you meet someone unexpectedly while in a hurry, ask the basics and then explain you're in a rush but are glad they are well/happy/planning a holiday, etc. Don't stand there tapping your toe and panicking.

◆ Don't introduce people as their nicknames, unless they never use anything else. And don't make any personal 'This is John, he's just got divorced' statements. That's their information to share.

◆ Don't let a door swing in someone's face – in fact, hold it open for them. If you get to a door at the same time as someone else, let them go first.

◆ Don't stroke a pregnant woman's stomach without asking.

◆ Falling over in the street is a mortifying experience... but try to laugh it off. Pick yourself up, check for broken heels, laddered tights and cuts or grazes, and have a giggle. You've just brightened up everyone's day.

◆ Being ill in public is always a nightmare, so if at all possible, stay at home. You don't want to risk vomiting or spluttering in public (I won't even mention the drama that is diarrhoea) and you won't get better while stressing over keeping it together. Also other people won't appreciate catching your illness and will blame you for it.

◆ Learning to bite your tongue is very useful. Yes, you're probably right, but the world isn't ready for your philosophy yet. Keep it for close friends.

◆ Never slap people unless they are having a coughing fit, trying to walk in front of oncoming traffic or putting their hand up your skirt. Girl fights and all the hair-pulling that comes with them look especially pathetic. A sharp turn on your heel makes a far more elegant statement.

◆ In short, treat everyone with respect – until they've proven to you they're not worth it. Let your manners speak for you and hopefully you'll get the same in return.

Chapter Two

Friendly *faux pas*

FRIENDS – THEY'RE GOOD for going shopping, eating chocolate, dancing, gossiping, watching videos, doing keep-fit, getting groomed and going on holiday with *and* they big you up and make you feel popular! Blood is thicker than water, though, so you can't get away with treating your friends the same way you would your relatives. They hang around because you are kind, funny, intelligent and honest – so don't become a bitch with an attitude problem and expect them to go along with it. Be nice, though, and the mates worth having will be there forever.

Ten commandments of friendship

1. Pick friends who make you feel good about yourself.

2. A jealous friend will never be an honest friend.

3. Trust your instincts. If a person genuinely likes you, you'll know.

4. New friends are just as valuable as old friends, for different reasons.

5. Don't ask a friend to do something you wouldn't want to do.

6. Respect the fact your friends have different priorities from yours.

7. Don't stew on an argument or cross word – sort it out.

8. Don't forget a friend's birthday.

9. Ring a friend if something big is happening in their life, even if it's for one minute.

10. Use your friends for support, but don't overburden them. Everyone has limits and their own lives to get on with.

How to be a cool companion

Even if you've grown up with someone, people change and develop in ways foreign to you. But even though you're married with a child and your schoolfriend is living with drag queens in Rio, you can still connect. The most important thing to do is never judge your friends by your own approach to life. They're different from you, which is why you find them so interesting. You might not approve of their partner, child's name, occupation or drinking habits, but they're not asking you to live that life. They just want you to be in it. Take a chill pill and your friendship has a much stronger chance of surviving.

Sometimes it is only right to interfere if you honestly feel a mate is about to make a huge mistake. I'm not talking about letting them go out in dangerously high heels looking like a slut, I'm talking about letting them date someone you know has been sleeping around, for example. If you feel a friend could be making a mistake due to depression, confusion or drunkenness, grab them by the hair and yell 'Nooooo!'

Of course, if they reject your advice you can't go on about it. Let it be and then look after them when they need your support because it's all gone wrong. Never say 'I told you so' (unless they are the kind of person who repeatedly makes the same silly mistakes and you want to give them a wake-up call). Work with their best interests at heart all the time and be there for them.

VIFs

Forget VIPs – Very Important Friends are what matters. And there are all kinds of mates for all kinds of occasions. Pick carefully from a wide platter and you'll have someone for every eventuality.

'The big sister'

This person can literally be your big sister, or older cousin, or any person of the same sex who's been there, done it, worn out the T-shirt and is happy to share her experiences with you. You may not want to take her advice, but having a friend from a slightly different generation will lend you support and brains – and you won't be competing because she's over that stage of her life. Future boyfriends are also more likely to be scared of her, which is no bad thing. And parents will feel happy you have a friend like that.

'The childhood friend'

You've known this person forever – you joked about in the playground, smoked your first cigarette together and chased around the boy band of the day in her first car. She (this far back it's likely to be a 'she' – you hated boys at primary school, remember?) reminds you who you are and where you came from. She knows a little too much about you and won't let you get away with anything – be careful when inviting her to work functions. But she'll be honest and loyal and having long-standing friends is a sign that you're doing OK. I worry when I meet people who haven't had anyone in their lives for longer than five years – either they're very annoying or very fickle.

'The new best friend'

This is someone who has come into your life quite unexpectedly – but wonderfully! Your love for them is almost romantic: they seem exciting, enlightened and full of good ideas. They can motivate you to try new things and see new places and they allow you to be who you want to be.

Don't go on too much to other friends about how cool this person is, though – it will get their backs up and it could just be a passing phase on your part. Remember to balance new friends with old friends – even try and introduce them – and enjoy the fact you can still attract such lovely folk.

'The male friend'

This could be a good mate, an old lover or a gay guy who is more of a girl than your girlfriends. Men bring many good things to a friendship: a different perspective, potential dates, knowledge of things you've never thought about and comfy jumpers. Just don't allow the male friend to be a platonic boyfriend if you're single. If there's no romantic inclination there, still go out with the girls to find Mr Right. If you go out sharking with your male friend, other men will be put off.

'The work friend'

Don't jump into friendships the first week in the office. You need to start slowly so you know who you can trust, who is good fun and who will be able to maintain a professional relationship when they have to. You don't want to get drunk and disorderly and then worry all weekend that your work buddy's on the phone to your boss.

'The boyfriend'

Don't lose sight of the fact that your partner is another friend. Partner etiquette demands that you should be mates too and be able to laugh, cry and give each other space when necessary. Of course, these things are all part of love, but there is a serious point to be made. Don't lose sight of the companionship and camaraderie that made you click in the first place and the effort you put in to win his love. It's all there in the name: boy*friend*.

Mixing groups

You love your friends; therefore they should love each other right? Wrong! You have different friends for different reasons – reasons that could easily wind up other mates.

When you do get them mixing, though, it can be wonderful. The main reason I had such a fantastic wedding day was because I walked into the church and saw my childhood friends chatting with university friends, and my cousins talking to my colleagues. So if you want to have all the people you love in a room together, here's how to handle it:

◆ Brief certain friends on things you're not keen for others to know.

◆ Try not to slag off one friend to another in the hope they'll never meet.

◆ Use yourself as a connecting tool, i.e. 'You both think I'm a bit too bossy. Discuss.' Play the fool if necessary.

◆ Don't push too hard for them to become good friends. As long as they're polite, be happy.

◆ If conversation is dwindling, move to the dance floor. Music is a great medium.

◆ Tell the other friends how you met this person. A background story will aid conversation.

◆ If you want a few very important friends to meet, arrange a special dinner at your place or a cocktail evening. It's hard to bond in a busy nightclub.

◆ In a formal situation, always sit your friends with at least one person they know. You can't force people to mix and they won't have a good time if they're stuck with strangers.

♦ Try to have equal numbers from different groups – don't have 20 university mates and one schoolfriend and expect the school chum to feel included.

♦ If two of your friends don't get on, don't force it. Include everyone in big events like your birthday night out, but don't be offended if one of them doesn't make it because the other will be there. Sometimes there are genuine reasons why they don't like each other and if you feel unable to take sides (sometimes you'll have to if a true injustice has been done), don't tell one of the friends all about your meetings with the other one.

♦ Booze is always helpful at getting people integrated, so pop the champagne.

How much time should you spend with your friends?

As your life develops, you have to make choices. You're no longer 15 years old with empty weekends for sloping around the town centre and eyeing up boys in McDonald's. Saturdays are now spent catching up on sleep, the laundry and your phone calls. Your career and romantic relationship need to be prioritised and in the few hours you're not thinking about them, it's quite nice to put your feet up with a box of chocolates and a good DVD. So when do you see your friends?

Well, the good news is that good friends are good friends and you can go for weeks, even months (sometimes years) without seeing them. The best thing to do is make sure it counts every time you do see them. Don't feel obliged to go along to a friend's work piss-up every Thursday – you know you won't get a quiet minute with them and you'll feel bad for going. Sometimes less is more. Admit to each other the weeks are getting booked up, so set a date in the future and do something special you can both really enjoy – book a fabulous restaurant, perhaps, or take a day trip together. I have friends I only see twice a year and there's no real excuse for it – we all live within miles of each other. But instead of feeling guilty or making lots of false plans which have to be cancelled at the last minute, we relish planning something quite lavish together – and always have a lot to talk about by the time our biannual catch-up occurs.

Some friends you will see more often. It's not that you like them more than the others, but maybe they live nearer, they're more flexible or they make more of an effort. I have a great bunch of mates who all go to the same gym as me. So in this fitness-conscious age we inspire ourselves to hit the aerobics class with the promise of a girlie chinwag in the jacuzzi afterwards. Another friend has started attending my photography classes, so I now have a set time to see her every week. Building each other into your schedules can really work. If you work in similar fields, meet for a semi-justified business lunch. If you've both moved away but your parents still live in the same village, arrange to go back home the same weekend.

If you sense a friend needs to see you more for any reason, make a few hours. It won't hurt you to miss the gym or your work night out for once. You may fancy a week of early nights, but a few late-night drinking sessions with a true mate won't do you too much damage.

However, if you don't see people as often as they'd like, don't be made to feel guilty. You are busy. You are popular. You are professional. As long as you are there when they need you – and you stay in touch with regular e-mails and phone calls – you're doing OK. If a friend moans too much about not seeing you, they'll soon become a bore and you'll want to see them even less. Be frank about your time restrictions and hopefully they'll understand. Just don't forget their birthday.

NB Bumping into an old mate can be weird – especially if you don't remember where you know them from. Be pleased and ask the basics, but don't pry too much. And don't feel the need to swap phone numbers and promise to see each other again. Give them a business card if you want, though, especially if you want to show off about your fab new job.

Friendship rules

If you haven't got anything nice to say...

However drunk, annoyed or blabber-mouthed you are, never snitch on a mate. It's an honour they've told you something private, so treat it with respect. And don't assume you can tell your mum/boyfriend either. If they asked you not to tell *anyone* they mean it. If you do let something slip, come clean. At least your friend will be prepared when someone says something about it. And don't expect to be trusted for a while – trust has to be earned.

And speaking of trust, betraying a mate for the sake of a cheap laugh will only cause long-term trouble. Bitchy chitchat about friends is one of the greatest pleasures in life ... but is a definite modern girl no-no. If you gossip about your friends to others, worst of all in the same group, the likelihood is they will gossip about you too. Even worse, you'll get a reputation for being insincere. You'll soon find that socially, being negative won't get you very far.

If a mate has annoyed you and you have to tell *someone*, use your partner or parents as a sounding-board. Remember, though, that mums and older friends remember everything.

Soul support

So let's dwell on the reverse side of gossip. Talk can be cheap, but a compliment from a friend can mean a great deal. If a friend has lost weight, got a nice tan or is wearing something that really suits them, tell them. If someone you know has said something nice about a friend, pass it on. If someone fancies one of your friends, tell them, it'll make their day (even if they are taken).

Invoking the mantra of etiquette – 'putting others before yourself' – it follows that a true friend deserves 100 per cent loyalty. Give them your complete backing when they're in trouble or hurt, and always take their side in an argument (even if they're being a little irrational). Stick up for each other. Make each other feel special.

JANE, 26

❛ I was put in an awful position last year when a friend started shagging another friend's boyfriend. I was equally close to both of them but I couldn't condone what was going on. Luckily, another acquaintance broke the bad news to my cuckolded mate and I was there for her 100 per cent. I would expect the same from my friends. My dirty ex-mate never forgave me, but she's still seeing the man, so I'm sure she thinks selling her soul was worth it. ❜

Soul support means you will be there for a friend. Never abandon a valued chum for someone new simply for the sake of change. And while we're on the subject, it's also great if you get on with your friend's friend. But not too much. Don't arrange nights out without your mutual mate and don't inform them of things *their* friend has been up to. That's just rude. If your mutual mate distances themselves over time, however, it's fine to start going out on your own.

Your relationship of trust, support and consideration also means you remember important dates, details about your friends' families and call them when they need to hear a friendly voice. By the same token, although spending an evening with a coughing, vomiting mess isn't your idea of a great night out, if a friend is on their own and needs company, grab a DVD and an anti-germ face mask and get round there. Holding someone's hair back while they vomit is a true test of friendship.

Fortunately, care and attention can also be shown by a small yet thoughtful present. Don't think of the price, think of the person.

A word of warning about possessions, though: don't assume you're so close that 'what's mine is automatically yours'. It's nice to share things but it's not nice to have to beg to get them back. The old saying 'Neither a borrower nor a lender be' makes a lot of sense. If someone damages or loses something special, you're bound to feel resentment and vice versa. If you lend someone money, don't feel bad about asking for it back, unless it's really small change. Think twice about lending anyone fairly large sums and be wary of people who repeatedly come to you for a handout.

Social butterflies

Out on the town together and looking hot to trot? Even if you pull a stunner, your single 'sister' is the first priority. Before you disappear into the night with Prince Charming, make sure she has safe transport, a mobile phone and enough cash to get home. If she's the worse for wear, go home with her and keep your man waiting.

If you fancy the same guy, maybe it's safer if neither of you goes for him. Your friendship is not worth a dispute over who gets to make the move. It's best to establish this simple ground rule at the beginning of the evening, before the alcohol takes hold. There is no dignity in a catfight while some smug guy looks on, pleased with all the attention. That being said, if it's clear your friend and the guy are genuinely interested in each other and you aren't in the running, is it really fair to sabotage possible true love because you saw him first?

Three's a crowd?

Having one best friend is easier socially than dealing in odd numbers. So don't be sensitive if you have two mates and they decide to do something without your involvement. You all have different interests and schedules, right? That being said, it doesn't mean that your feelings should not be considered. If they decide to go out to the theatre together, you should be invited to go to the pop concert the following week. Make sure you get together as a threesome regularly – and that you tease each other in equal amounts.

Along similar lines, if you don't share social interests with a friend, consider putting yourself out once in a while. Hopefully they'll do the same and attend that wrestling match with you!

But if you are on your own without a partner in crime,

enjoy the solitude and go with the flow. As long as you're safe, as a modern girl you should feel comfortable out and about in society and shouldn't expect anyone to bat an eyelid. There is absolutely no stigma in sitting alone in a café reading a book or even, heaven forbid, going to the cinema and asking for just one ticket.

Balancing boyfriends

Love is a many-splendoured thing... but not for the friend who's pushed out when Mr Wonderful shows up. Remember the following:

1. Unless this one is your future husband, your friend will be around much longer.

2. Your friend can give you valuable feedback and advice.

3. The first flushes of love soon calm down and then you'll need someone to go shopping with.

4. You wouldn't like to be pushed to one side for a man, would you?

5. You'll need someone to moan to when he starts snoring.

6. If your friend's single and lonely, don't give out all your fairytale details.

7. *No one* wants to know how big his willy is.

Why do you annoy your friends?

Yes, you're fabulous – but all modern girls can be a little too self-interested. Your friends love you (that's a given) but they don't always want to hear about how everyone fancies you, your new promotion or to act as your personal assistant-cum-taxi driver. Show off to your mum instead. Indulge her need for parental pride. You'll be surprised how many stories of your success she'll listen to (and bore the neighbours with, when you've gone).

Olive branches

If you really have damaged a friendship, mending it is easy – if you wholeheartedly want to… A few tips:

1. Ask your friend over for dinner and cook their favourite things – it shows you want to treat them and make them feel cared for.

2. Send them a card for no reason other than you love them.

3. Go on a friends' holiday – even if it's just a night away in the country.

4. Book the afternoon off work, take a leisurely lunch and treat your friend to something they adore.

5. Say sorry. And mean it.

Ending a friendship

Sometimes friendships do turn sour and when the bad times start to outweigh the good, it's time to leave. Friends are there to offer support, security and a social life, and a good friend will make you feel happy, popular and loved. When a friend starts to suck the life out of you, drag you down and make you feel bad about yourself, it's time to get ditching.

MOLLY, 31

   6 For a good few years, I was chummy with a girl from university. She was always a bit odd – she fancied all the same men as me, she would be sarcastic about my taste in clothes and often blow me out for other people at the last minute. When I started meeting nicer people who asked about me, invited me to things and encouraged me to feel confident in myself, I thought, "Is this normal?" I realised that friends should make you feel positive and so I faded the old friend out. She didn't like it because she needed me more than I needed her in the end. 9

Five easy steps to ditching a bitch:

1. Stop returning the calls and e-mails. Harsh but swift.

2. Get busy – start going out with new buddies and you won't notice the old friend's not there.

3. Don't feel bad. You're a decent person; you wouldn't be doing this if your friend weren't a pain in the ass.

4. Have it out with them. If they're not getting the hint, tell them a few home truths – but expect to hear a few in return. Be fair and diplomatic: admit you're not perfect but you do expect honesty/loyalty/kindness.

5. If they get in contact some time later, reconsider your stance. But as soon as their old characteristics rear their ugly head, don't waste any time getting out.

At other times, it's no one's fault, but people just change and grow apart. This is sad, but means you've matured and distancing yourself from that friendship shows you're ready to move on and make friends with people you have more in common with. Don't flog a dead horse. It's better to remember a friend fondly than resent spending a night with them instead of your partner or your wonderful new friends.

Secrets of Success

◆ If you're a woman's woman, don't be ashamed of it. Girls who are afraid to hang around with their own gender are often insecure or just plain jealous. Hanging out with the boys or being a ladette doesn't make you any cooler.

◆ Even if you don't have anything of value to say to a friend in need, offer a shoulder to cry on and an ear to bend.

◆ When you are suggesting a get-together with a good pal, remember they may not be earning as much as you or feel comfortable in the same places. Pick somewhere both of you will enjoy.

◆ If you do earn more than a friend, don't feel you have to buy bigger presents or pick up the cocktail bill every time you go out. Your friend should be happy you're doing so well and not expect anything more than your time. If you really are more comfortable, surprise her with the odd treat.

◆ If you lend something to a mate, be prepared for it to get broken, lost or ruined – and you can't hold it against them forever. However, they should return things and you shouldn't feel bad about reminding them. It must have been something you loved or you wouldn't have been so keen for them to watch/read/wear it, right?

- If you have borrowed something and had an accident, 'fess up. Offer to replace it or pay for dry-cleaning. Your friend will probably say 'no worries', but at least you offered. It's all about respect.

- Sometimes your best intentions are way off and a friend won't like a gift you've chosen. If they say so, don't be offended. Be happy they feel comfortable enough to tell you, give them the receipt and even suggest you go shopping together to buy a replacement.

- Don't feel obliged to get too close too quickly. Your new buddy might be the type to have a mate-a-minute and share personal info with all and sundry. You don't have to fill them in on your menstrual cycle and favourite sexual position if you don't want to. You can be fond of someone without describing your nipples.

- If a friend has a new fella, there is every possibility you won't like him quite as much as she does. You might not be able to stand him. But be polite. If she asks you directly what you think of him, throw in a few positives ('He obviously loves his mum, so he must respect women') before you list the bad things. And don't go overboard. If she really likes him, criticising him could cost you the friendship.

- On the other hand, if a friend can't stand your bloke – and you know it – don't let it get you down. Ask why and if there's no justification for it, leave it. They just clash. If your friend does have a good reason (he speaks to you badly, for example), think about it. After all, your friends should have your best interests at heart.

- When you get serious with a bloke, some of your male friends will find it hard to take. It's not always because they were secretly hoping you'd one day see the light and run to their arms – it's sometimes because they don't think much of your choice or they liked being the only bloke on the block. Understand if they disappear for a bit when they get a new bird too.

- If a friend asks you to be a bridesmaid, witness or reader at their wedding, or a godmother to their child, be grateful. This is indeed an honour and your friend will have thought carefully about the best person for the job. Even if you think marriage is archaic and children are foul, it means a lot to your friend, so it should mean a lot to you too.

- Your relationship with your girlfriends will change when they settle down with someone, get married and/or have babies. You may think they've got boring but if they're happy, they're happy. Try not to judge. They may not be up for a girlie tour to Tenerife anymore, but they might be the best friends to go to the theatre or for a walk in the park with. Still, remember that just because a friend has a partner/husband/baby they don't have to join her every time you meet up. Insist on some girl-only nights. It'll do your friend as much good as it will you and your friendship. Circumstances change, but friends can be there forever.

Chapter Three

The art of conversation

W HOEVER SAID SILENCE is golden was talking absolute tosh. What you have to say for yourself will distinguish you from the crowd. There's no quicker method of making new friends, winning respect and getting things done your way.

Who, where, what, when...

Before you agree (or are forced) to go somewhere, find out who will be there and what kind of occasion it is. If you're tired, premenstrual or just not in the mood, it's sometimes better not to go somewhere filled with strangers you have to impress. To make 'good chat' you have to be feeling sociable and relatively confident. The following events can be quite a drain, especially when nervous:

- Work dos: a work do might be a good time to talk to your boss about how wonderful you are but it can be a long night if you're stuck with boring clients or people determined to 'talk shop'.

- Family dos: not so bad if you've seen each other recently. If not, it'll bring on a headache just trying to remember the names of all their children, grandchildren, etc.

- Parties: if you're single and on the pull, you'll be nervously anticipating a night of flirting and possible romance. If you're coupled up, being in a room where everyone's on the prowl can be depressing and boring (intellectual chitchat is out the window). The music may also make conversation impossible, as will alcohol after midnight.

- Dinner parties: being the polite, socially acceptable modern girl you are, no doubt the hostess has put you next to the painfully shy woman or the loutish oaf she knows only you would be able to handle. Sad but true – if you're wonderful, life often hands you the short social straw.

> **SAM, 33**
>
> ❛ I had a really embarrassing moment at a mothers and toddlers church group where all the mothers are terribly polite, etc. One of the women asked if I would like a coffee and I offered to give her a hand, as you do. As soon as the words came out of my mouth I looked down and realised that she only had one hand. If that was not bad enough, when she said she was alright and went off into the kitchen I turned around and all the other mums were in hysterics. ❜

Body talk

Before you start worrying about *what* to say, think about what your face and body are saying. Your appearance will make a more dramatic impression than your first word – unless you have a comical voice.

When you say 'hello', maintain eye contact (only for three seconds then look away if you're trying to flirt) and smile. Yes, that's right, make like a swan – look serene and and confident and people won't know that underneath the water the legs are paddling madly trying to keep you afloat. Give yourself the air of a happy, important person and people should treat you as such. Handy hints:

◆ Smile smart. Smile genuine. Don't grin like a goon with your hands on your hips. People can pick out fakes, and insincerity can make anyone feel uncomfortable.

◆ Keep eye contact throughout your chat, but don't stare too intently. You'll scare people. Or look confrontational.

♦ Don't cross your arms, turn your back to someone while they're still talking, shake your head at what they're saying or yawn. This behaviour is very discouraging for the person trying to communicate. Obviously.

Making contact

Location, location, location

Informal conversations in public places, e.g. in the supermarket queue or sitting on the bus, are often the trickiest to handle, especially if the person who has struck up the chat is a complete stranger. Be guided by their tone and your surroundings. Keep it simple and don't be afraid to match like with like until you feel more relaxed. 'Yes, I know what you mean' or 'It *is* freezing, isn't it?' Most of all, listen carefully, as you won't be used to the person's inflection or tone.

In other social environments – visits to other people's homes, restaurants, bars or clubs and, sometimes, within the workplace – it is always handy to have a few fallback conversation options. If you dry up quicker than a puddle in the Sahara, ponder, but don't over-practise, the ideas below. If you're not worried about what to say but merely when or how, you can skip the next bit.

Foolproof conversation starters

People like to talk about themselves and hear views about what's going on in the world, trivial and otherwise. If you go to any social gathering with a moderately nosy nature and a story about a celebrity, you should be welcomed. Good advice here is to buy a newspaper before venturing out and read up on what's going on in the world. Other good topics include…

◆ **The weather:** it's not boring, sometimes it just has to be discussed. Even chatting about the rain to close friends and family (lucky them!) can be worthwhile. You'll be surprised how quickly it leads into broader conversations about social plans and holidays.

◆ **Physical attributes:** if someone has lost weight or got a new haircut, mention it. Even if they just look generally well, ask them what they've been up to. Let's hope it wasn't a quick shag that put a glow in their cheeks. Be careful about commenting about someone's appearance to someone else – it can easily seem as if you're gossiping and people may hear sarcasm when in fact you were being entirely positive.

◆ **The venue:** 'Have you been here before?' is a great opener, as are 'Where are the loos?' and 'I love this wall-paper, do you?' Remember questions demand an answer and are the fastest route to a two-way exchange.

◆ **Their children:** however boring you think the 'mini-thing' is, the parents could discuss its teething, nappy-doings and first words for hours. If you're stuck, get them going and watch them run … and just 'aah' at regular intervals.

◆ **An elaborate lie:** it will get everyone's attention, even if they later kick you out when you admit you're not *actually* Tom Jones's lovechild.

◆ **The host:** even if you have nothing else in common, someone must have invited you. Ask about how they know them – hopefully they'll say something interesting for you to grasp on to.

◆ **The job:** at work, getting a conversation underway can be easily achieved by discussing what you're there for. Ask for or offer to help with work or equipment and before you know it you'll feel comfortable in taking the conversation further.

◆ **A simple introduction:** go on, try it, just introduce yourself. 'Hi. My name is so and so.' Just remember to avoid the modern curse of introducing yourself with 'So what do you do?' No one likes to be defined by their status unless they are extremely egotistical.

Wherever you are, don't be afraid to admit you don't know anyone, you're shy or you're nervous. Go on search of someone who also seems to on their lonesome. If at a party, position yourself by the buffet table to catch passers-by for a chinwag over the cheese straws. Don't linger around the loos (you'll look like a perv!), but do escape to a cubicle for a few minutes' breather if you've run out of things to say to your new acquaintance.

Social small talk

The opening exchanges are now a distant memory and you're an active participant in the social world. But at parties, bars or clubs you don't necessarily want to share your life history with every Tom, Dick and Harry. You just want to pass a few hours. This is where small talk comes in. Yes, it can be superficial, but it is also extremely useful.

As well as being interesting in its own right, this miniconflab should establish:

1. Who's who.

2. Who to avoid.

3. Who to talk to next.

When making small talk socially, avoid the following topics (at least until you've all had a few drinks or know each other better): politics, religion, salaries, breast implants, cellulite, hairy bits, manufactured boy bands, your garden shed, verrucas, Afghanistan and soap operas. You'll either bore/scare the poor gimps to death or come across as a vacuous bimbo. Once you're past the introductions, you can ask: 'What do you do for a living?' It's (usually) an interesting topic and (always) says a lot about the person you're chatting to.

In small talk, the following is mandatory: don't dominate, always listen and never jump into somebody else's sentence because you think you know what they are going to say or want to agree with them.

And remember, sometimes people simply don't want to talk or may have other things on their mind. If you're getting no response, don't push it, just move on.

CLAIRE, 28

❝ I don't know about you, but I find it so irritating when strangers (read "builders", "shop assistants") deign to say: "Smile, it may never happen." How presumptuous! For all they know, "it" may already have happened. And why should I muster up an expression of happiness just to make them feel better? Smiles are infectious and the best way to receive a smile is give one. ❞

Getting to know you....

So you feel comfortable with the person you're talking to. You've moved on from chitchat to meaningful conversation... but the etiquette pitfalls are still there.

Any nosy parker faced with your glorious being will want to know all about you. Don't feel inclined to open up completely – especially in front of the boss's wife or your husband's new business partner. Even through an alcoholic haze, you must try to keep your embarrassment reflex active. My husband once embarked on a jolly little debate about our contraceptive methods in front of an unsuitable audience. He got a serious telling off when he got home. Where was his reflex? If you've embarked on a particular topic and any member of your circle starts coughing nervously or twitching erratically, you've gone too far. Zip it.

You should also refrain from emotional subjects if there's something you haven't got a handle on yet. It takes a long time to get over divorce, death and depression (and numerous other serious issues), so if someone asks you about it – however politely – and you're not ready to talk, don't get pushed into it. It could spoil the evening if you burst into tears and run out of the room – not only for you but for the person who asked the question and for the host. You'd also worry about people talking about you afterwards, thinking you're a fruit-loop, etc. Instead of getting sucked in, try a curt, 'Sorry, I'm not ready to talk about that' or 'Oh, don't ask – shall I get us a refill?' This also applies if a subject is brought up that you have extreme emotional views on. Sometimes it's better to politely withdraw than risk a full-on clash. Decide whether it's really worth it.

Off-limits

In conversation, you don't have to put up with anything you're not comfortable with. Remember:

1. You don't have to tell your real age if you don't want to (although that's very old skool – be proud of your years).

2. Never feel obliged to reveal your weight. Give your dress size if you wish.

3. Medical history is nobody else's business.

4. Distributing your e-mail address or phone number is not a 'Get Out Quick' card – it will haunt you later and be far more difficult to overcome than working out how to say 'no'.

5. Your partner's penis is not a subject for open debate.

Personal space

Don't invade it. Apart from the occasional lean in when the music is too loud, keep a decent gap between yourself and your companion. You might feel OK with a stranger hanging on to your shoulders and chinking glasses every two seconds, but many find it creepy. If you do feel that your own space is being violated, take a step back. If the other person follows you, hold your drink out in front of you (especially if it's red wine) as a block.

Circulating

However much fun you're having with the vicar and his lady wife, it's important at social events to keep moving and introducing yourself – especially at a work function or in a room filled with people you haven't seen for a while. But don't shark the room. People will be aware you're only fulfilling a function before you move on and serious networkers often come across as being desperate and hard-nosed. No, rather than sharking, move around the food and drinks area, escape losers, spend longer with nice folk, and ask the host if there is anyone in particular they would like you to meet.

How to talk to...

For some reason, when a certain person sidles up to you it is impossible to know what to say. I'm not talking about the shy guys or girls, who are, generally, happy to listen to you waffling on about the size of your sofa for half an hour rather than talk themselves, I'm talking about the ones who want to chat but somehow you just can't find the right words with which to respond.

Children

Children are easy if you're comfortable. Some people have an inbuilt fear of all things under four foot (and kids do vomit, scream and wee unexpectedly, so who can blame them?) but treat them like mini-adults and you'll both be happy. I don't mean debate local politics or ask about work, I mean avoid baby voices and patronising questions. Talk about music, television programmes and Harry Potter and you're sure to find a bond.

Teenagers

These are trickier, because they pretend they don't want to talk. They want you to think they'd rather be burning in hell, or at least in their darkened bedroom smoking weed, than at this motley event with you nerds. But if you ignore them, they'd feel left out. Rule number 1? Just be normal, don't pressure them and never, ever try to be cool – they can spot it a mile off. See Ben Stiller in *Meet the Parents* if you need convincing.

The elderly

They have, by their very definition, lived and seen more than you can imagine. Don't assume they're past it and have nothing to tell you. We're only able to be modern girls because of the effort a lot of them put in. Therefore etiquette is never ageist. Ask about grandchildren, their neighbours, what they used to do for a living – and then get them onto interesting subjects like what they got up to during the world wars, or what they thought of the 1960s sexual revolution.

A word of realistic advice: don't automatically assume that an older person will understand your friendly intentions. Different generations invariably find it hard to understand each other's behaviour. Take extra care with older people and be that bit more considerate, and you won't go far wrong.

Foreigners

Foreigners are limited on the conversation front because English-speakers are generally so bad at learning other languages, yet in the modern world it's a huge no-no to not even try to meet people halfway. If you can't manage a few phrases of someone's language, at least praise their country if you have been there and find out more if your haven't (but don't ask daft questions like 'Do you know my cousin who lives in the mountains?' or 'Do you have electricity where you're from?') Be patriotic but never racist or nationalistic, and answer any questions they have about your country.

DONNA, 23

❝ An old auntie of mine always makes me cringe in public. She's so proud of being Italian – although she's lived in the UK for half her life – she says things like "Tut, tut, the English are so bad at cooking!" when we take her to a friend's house for dinner. She also talks loudly as if all English people are stupid, and comments on the poor style of passers-by in the street. Luckily she's getting on a bit, so new people put it down to age. It's just my family that knows she's always been out of control. ❞

Celebrities

Celebrities can leave you awestruck. Yes, yes, you've seen them on the telly but they really are just like you and me … just a little more self-obsessed. If you happen to stumble across one, act like a journalist and ask them non-probing, positive questions about themselves. Throw in a few bizarre stories of your own and they'll soon warm to you. It'll be nice for them to hear about 'the real world' and all that malarkey. And don't lick arse. The sad ones might expect it, but you'll come away feeling daft, and the really talented stars don't need it.

In this fame-obsessed age it's perfectly fine to ask for an autograph or a photo, but remember they are human and have privacy rights too. Use your head and your heart.

The language of love

Talking of hearts, conversation can be even more tricky when romance is on the agenda. Before we look at how to navigate this minefield, there's a very simple rule: 'no' means 'no' and 'yes' means 'yes'. If a social occasion becomes one-to-one, then make sure you're fully aware of what you are getting into. Language can be very persuasive, but can also send all of the wrong signals. 'Coming up for a coffee' doesn't always imply a caffeine-break.

As the relationship develops or ends, be mindful that it's only fair your language should always be clear and honest. Not only will it protect your own heart, but you're less likely to break anyone else's. Men may be idiots some of the time but you should seek to use words to respect, reassure and contact them in much the same way that you would like to be treated.

The morning after

If you find yourself waking up in someone else's flat with a raging hangover and are lost for words (or any good reason why you are there), don't be a bitch. It's the modern girl's right to behave freely but not to disregard good manners. By all means dash out mortified, if you must, but leave a note or make a polite excuse for your rapid departure.

Pet names

Under no circumstances use pet names in public when addressing your partner. Not only will you come across as a bewilderingly pathetic creature, but you risk making those without their own 'liddle flumeky bumpkin' sad, lonely and then angry. It's especially hard to maintain any street cred when referring to yourself as a 'trixie rabbit'. Of course sometimes you will slip up. The occasional lapse can be endearing, but anything more is very bad form.

Talking yourself out of trouble

Sometimes, free-flowing banter isn't, er, free-flowing. But however difficult or embarrassing a conversation, there are ways of handling those 'death would be easier' moments.

You can't think of anything to say... so don't! Leave it up to the other person. A conversation is a two-way thing and if you've made an effort and they haven't responded, the onus is on them. If you're a kind soul, help them out with questions which require long answers: 'Tell me about your wedding' or 'What changes have you made to your house since you've been there?' Something as basic as 'I love your earrings – where are they from?' can fill a few minutes.

Even worse than the person who won't talk is the one who won't stop. We've all been there – that moment when the most boring person in the world becomes your new best friend. Now, madam, be polite – don't yawn, look at your nails or turn away. And making excuses like going to the buffet could give them the excuse to join you. Subtly look around for someone to pounce on, even if it's just to add someone a bit sparkier to your current *tête-à-tête*. When push comes to shove, say forcefully, 'It's been nice talking to you. I should go now and mingle. Goodbye.' Looking on the bright side, being bored will sober you up quickly and give you time to plan this week's shopping.

But what to do when *you're* the one with a motor mouth? You've rambled on for an age like the village idiot... and you can't seem to stop! Yikes, take a breather before it's too late. Trying to cover too much ground too quickly is a common mistake. It all comes back to our natural reflex to fill a silence. Nice people will realise you're nervous and help you out, even if it involves silencing you with gaffer tape. You'll be grateful in the morning.

Gaffer tape can also seem like a useful tool when confronted with a foul-breathed ogre snuggling in for a long chat... Pongo city! Even worse, they spit when they talk and there's a piece of salami stuck on their tooth. What do you do? Offer a mint or chewing gum if you have it (after taking one yourself of course), or suggest trying a cocktail (the stronger the better). To avoid the waterfall, move sideways on, pretending to peruse the room with them (this should also help with the breath thang because now it makes sense to only offer your ear when talking). And it is only a kindness to tell them about that salami. You'd want to know, wouldn't you?

When attraction becomes an issue, the art of conversation becomes very clouded. This is worse if you're not the one falling in love. Let's look at an example: a complete nightmare is coming on to you but, not wanting to come across as big-headed, you don't do a runner. It's not so bad. After all, he's single and mentioned a nice flat and his football prowess. You're starting to look beyond his appearance when things quickly take a turn for the worse. He's whispering into your ear about the size of his member, and it's too late – you're well and truly stuck with him. Except that you're not. Start by praising your boyfriend – even if you haven't got one. Maybe state politely, 'You're not my type, but that woman over there has been looking your way all night.' Putting yourself first is the last resort of etiquette, but if necessary, get someone else in trouble! If the man doesn't take these hints, do a runner. Go to the bar, grab a passer-by or hide in the loos for a bit. If the worst comes to the worst, say your goodbyes and leave completely. You won't enjoy yourself lurking behind the curtains.

In reverse, here's how to handle it when a handsome hunk is coming on to you: wa-hey! If you're up for it, get the banter going. Keep it light, fun and flirty. *Don't* suggest you go off to a hotel room there and then. Enjoy the conversation, use the time to find out more about him and coyly reveal your best. And offer him your e-mail address or work number at the end of your chat. That's girl power.

HILARY, 31

❝ An old boss of mine was quite a woman. She would glide into a party and whisper to me, "I'm tired, so I'm only going to stay for an hour." Even though she wasn't staying long, she'd check in her coat and bag so people didn't know and she could move freely. When she spoke to people, she smiled, made eye contact and remembered seemingly irrelevant details that made them feel special. I'm sure everyone she spoke to felt like a million dollars, even though she just made small talk for a few minutes. She didn't waste time at the buffet or queuing for drinks and the next morning she would always say it was nice just to check in with people while I was nursing a hangover and cringing over what I might have said. ❞

'Did I really say that?'

We've all been there, embarrassed the next day by something we said or did. Especially if alcohol has been involved. If you did say anything too cringy, don't let it eat you up. If someone mentions it, don't get too defensive: you did it, after all! But if they continue to take the mickey weeks later, just remind them they've probably done it too, you're embarrassed enough and you'd be grateful if they dropped it.

If you're worried that you've offended someone, never sit it out and expect the problem to go away. Get in touch as soon as possible and apologise. However, a good rule to recall is that if you were drunk, chances are that a fair few of the other guests were too. They might remember less than you!

Public speaking

Eek! How scary. Standing up in front of a sea of bored or – even worse – enthusiastic faces can make you want to vomit and hide at the same time. But as times change, there are more and more arenas in which us girls are expected to command a room. You may find yourself standing at the top of the boardroom table (rather than taking notes in the corner) or addressing a crowd with a thoroughly modern chief bridesmaid's speech. Whatever, with a bit of help, you can get through it – and be a success. Just remember the following:

1. Be prepared. Familiarise yourself with the room well beforehand.

2. Use cards to talk from but have the full speech written out too (for emergencies).

3. Keep eye contact with a friendly face at the front to steady your nerves.

4. Don't try and be too funny – a few jokes at the start will suffice.

5. Don't worry about going red or stumbling over your words – chances are, the people listening to you won't have noticed.

6. Keep it short and make it relevant – the fewer tangents, the better.

7. Make it personal where possible – it will be easier to remember that way.

8. Slow it down – you may want to get off the stage, but you also want people to hear you.

9. Don't try to shock – and be politically correct (you don't want complaints).

10. Remember, it's not that important to anyone else – they're probably thinking about their next meal.

Secrets of Success

◆ Use a person's name in conversation – it shows you've remembered and are focusing on them.

◆ Don't talk with your mouth full.

◆ It's a human instinct to give a new person 30 seconds to impress you. But give people a few extra minutes. Nerves can make us all go a bit off-track and they could be wonderful.

◆ Don't offer people your business card in the first minute. It's like saying, 'I'm really important and you're really important

– let's use each other.' Wait and see if you actually get on or the card will be thrown straight in the bin.

◆ Don't just talk. Listen. Respond intelligently. Don't have the conversation set in stone before it takes place – the person could take you off in a more interesting direction if you go with the flow.

◆ Judge the mood. Don't moonwalk into a quiet huddle of friends singing 'Billie Jean'. Use your sixth sense.

◆ It's fine to earwig other conversations – we're all nosy – but don't interrupt and admit it. 'Oh, I just heard you're looking for a new flat, well...' That's too rude.

◆ Everyone has a specialist subject, even the most boring people in the world. They'll drop a few hints in the first few minutes about their preferred topic, so if things get really dull, force yourself to ask, 'So just how many trains have you spotted this year?' At least they'll be happy.

◆ Don't interview someone. Ask them questions, but allow them to answer without interrupting, don't get personal and take 'no' for an answer. Some things are better left unsaid. They're not applying for a job, they're trying to find the toilets.

◆ When a third person joins the conversation, fill them in on what you're discussing and ask the person talking to repeat 'the funny story about...' This will make the newcomer feel accepted and the old-talker feel wanted.

◆ Don't ask a complete stranger what they think of you or your plans. What can they say? They don't know you, so you won't get an honest or researched answer. It will also make you appear friendless and needy.

♦ Don't use clever-clever words. They never work in day-to-day conversation and will make you sound like a clever clogs who spends evenings in with the dictionary. If you genuinely use such words, fair enough, just make sure you are using them in context and they are not so obscure the listener is left feeling rather stupid or confused.

♦ Never use street language, code or cockney rhyming slang. Very sad.

♦ Don't use the word 'we' when you've just met someone. You don't know them and they'll wonder to whom you are referring.

♦ The best way to have something interesting to talk about... is to do something interesting, away from your job, your partner and your family, even if it's just taking photographs, studying yoga or gardening. Get busy.

Chapter Four

Work it, baby

GOOD MANNERS EACH DAY help you work, rest and play! Oh yes. Working isn't just about making a living – it's about making new friends, improving your future, getting an education, impressing others and getting out of the house. How can we do all that without getting anyone's back up? Easy…

Getting a job

Letting the world know that you are ready, willing and able for employment can be a tricky business. There's lots of competition out there and companies can afford to have the highest standards. So don't let yourself down at the first hurdle of what can be a fairly long race. Effective presentation of yourself and all your *appropriate* assets is the key to getting through that door.

Selling yourself

The interview is not the first chance you have to demonstrate your impeccable capability. Almost as important are your curriculum vitae and the letter of application you write to get you there in the first place. Check and check again for spelling and punctuation mistakes. Print on good-quality and possibly eye-catching paper. Get the recruitment official's name and title right. Don't lie on your CV (people do check) and don't list too many personal interests (who cares if you like new age cinema, one assumes all modern girls have many depths). A CV should be a maximum of two sheets of A4 paper, no longer. It's supposed to be a tempting insight into your history and the official proof of your suitability for the job, not a lonely hearts ad and therapist's report rolled into one.

Exclusive interviews

Before you can spend your first month's salary, you need to get the job. With many wonderful modern girls out there, competition in the job market is tough. Shine like a star, honey. Shine on. This is difficult because interviews are scary and it's hard to be yourself – especially when you really, really want the job. But interviews don't have to be impossible. Countless surveys of personnel managers and recruitment consultants say interviewees should just be prepared and be themselves. The following tips will help as well:

1. Arrive on time – preferably with five minutes to spare for a quick trip to the loo for a make-up, armpit and toilet check.

2. First impressions count. It's a fact that people decide whether they like a person in the first five minutes of meeting them. So be clean and don't smell. Don't look overtly sexual and don't wear things that make too much noise. Novelty items, such as parrot earrings and musical socks, will make you look like a weirdo.

3. Find out as much as you can about the department, the company, the industry and the competition. Knowledge is power, especially when you're trying to impress someone who works in that field.

4. Be confident – know your strengths – but don't be arrogant. You're not Little Miss Perfect of Perfect Town. No one likes a know-all, especially your future boss.

5. Imagine yourself through the interviewer's eyes. Are you being enthusiastic? Is your body language encouraging? Remember to smile, have a firm handshake, lean forward, maintain eye contact and walk with conviction – the interview starts the minute you walk into the room.

6. Interviewers always ask if you have any questions. Say something. If you ask nothing, they'll think you're a bit dumb. Plump for a simple question about holiday entitlement, bonuses, the team, your boss or main competitors if necessary.

7. As you leave, thank the interviewer(s) for their time, shake their hands firmly (not like a vice, though), and leave at speed. Don't hang about using your mobile or sorting out your handbag.

8. Don't be surprised to be called back for a second interview – and treat it as being as important as the first. You've impressed, but not enough. There's still a lot to prove.

9. If you get a letter saying you haven't got the job, do write back asking where you could improve. Most employers will be pleased to help you out. And don't feel too disheartened. Everything happens for a reason. A better job must be around the corner. And you never know, another opening may appear and they'll remember you.

10. If they contact you to say you've got the job, clever you. Read the contract carefully and compromise on a starting date as soon as possible. Research the position and the team you'll be part of. If you can, take a few days off between jobs to get your hair done and buy a new outfit. The night before, go to bed early. Take a herbal sleeping pill if it helps. Work out your route beforehand and leave 30 minutes early in case of delays.

Working girl

First-day nerves

Meeting so many new people while appearing professional – and working a new fax machine – can be difficult. But no one expects too much and you won't be weighed down with deadlines on the first day, so spend the time remembering names and places (it's very important to find the loos and the water cooler). You may be whisked off to a health and safety briefing (try not to laugh at the '70s home video about falling over a wastepaper basket) or to human resources to discuss pensions (interesting!), but ultimately you've got to bond with your new colleagues.

Get an overall feel for everyone and if you're crippled with shyness, tell people you're a little nervous – the kind ones will be keen to help. Make sure you eat breakfast and lunch. When you make tea, offer to make some for those around you. Leave when the others start drifting out and say goodbye to all those left.

Do not spend your first day flirting, gossiping, arse-licking, buddying up with one person, e-mailing friends, painting your nails, taking a long lunch break or thinking you made a mistake. All new places take time to get used to. Give it a week and it'll feel almost like home. You won't feel so self-conscious every time you ask a question and you should have a vague idea what you're there for.

Making yourself invaluable

Don't wait for others to set your standards – do it yourself. Be punctual, conscientious, polite and helpful. And be dedicated – it may not be your dream job but you should treat it as such.

One life lesson sticks clearly in my mind. My first job was at a fashion magazine as a beauty assistant. I was 21 and enthusiastic, but my heart was still a million miles away at university. My friends and I had planned a big reunion back on campus on a Monday night, so knowing it would be a late one (understatement of the year), I asked my formidable boss if I could come in an hour later than usual. She replied, 'Do you want to be a journalist? If you do, you'll make the right decision.'

In one sense, this put a dampener on things. I went out, drank a little and somehow ended up at work 30 minutes earlier than usual. On my desk was a box of chocolates and a card saying, 'I knew you'd make the right decision.' And I had. Even though my boss appeared three hours later after a leisurely breakfast with a famous composer, she'd earned the right to, I hadn't. This taught me early on that respect is earned and that in work hours you have to put work first if you want to make an impact.

Being a cool colleague

You probably spend more time with your colleagues than your loved ones. It's a sickening thought, isn't it? You didn't choose these people, they didn't choose you – and some days you fantasise about stapling the secretary's ears back or whacking your boss's head with your clip file. But in a bid to get along reasonably well...

♦ Keep your hands off others' mugs, staplers, scissors, personal photographs, cuddly toys (why do some women feel the need to have a cheeky chimp sitting on their computer?), mouse mats and paperclips. Ask before you borrow and return everything to its rightful place as soon as you've finished with it.

♦ Treat the office as you would your home and tidy all communal areas. Don't leave your lunch plate in the kitchen sink as if it will wash itself. Likewise, don't leave things in the fridge to produce a ghastly whiff.

♦ Don't call people sitting at the desk opposite you. Your other colleagues will feel suspicious and left out. If it's that personal, e-mail it and no one will ever know. Whispering and offices don't mix.

♦ Never resort to physical violence. Make your point through your line manager, or directly to the defendant if you catch them in a reasonable mood.

◆ Don't openly apply for jobs in front of your boss or your colleagues. It's disloyal, breaks up the team and highlights the fact you're not actually doing any work.

◆ Use the Internet and e-mail by all means. But try and do a little bit of work too. Remember they can see what you're doing. Think twice before sending on any attachments/dodgy e-mails.

◆ The weekend starts on Friday night, not Thursday lunchtime. Sure, drinking midday is fun, but only if you can handle it. Falling asleep on your keyboard is so 1985.

◆ If you're going to be in late, ask your boss's permission – and inform the person who'll be expected to cover your phone/work. Thank them afterwards.

◆ Don't loudly complain that your last office was much more fun. Or the men there were much more attractive.

◆ Don't suffer from Prince Charles syndrome and get over-attached to the plants. The human office inhabitants deserve the best position near the windows; don't fight for your cactuses.

◆ Dress appropriately. No fanny pelmets, boob tubes or see-through shirts. You are not Bridget Jones. You're a professional with a true sense of self. God forbid you should flash your *whatever* when you're replenishing the paper in the photocopier. Look as smart as the job permits and you'll earn respect and feel confident.

◆ Modern etiquette demands an active contribution when the collection plate goes round for someone's special birthday or leaving day. These should always be private and up to an individual to decide. Never berate another for their apparent thriftiness – you don't know their personal circumstances. Just do what you feel comfortable with and be honest if you can't take part.

HENRIETTA, 30

❝ There was a survey quite recently which stated work colleagues are increasingly pissed off that people don't say "Good morning, how was your weekend?", which I also think is crucial. Luckily, I work in a very nice place full of nice people, but without sounding sexist, it's no surprise that it's a 90 per cent female office – that does make a difference. ❞

The hours

Lunchtime is a tricky affair in the office because some people – normally your boss – will see a sandwich and a bit of fresh air as a sign of weakness and stay strapped to their desk for the duration. That's their choice. You're entitled to a break and it will make you much perkier in the afternoon. Plus, eating at your desk has been proven to give you indigestion. Don't be 'guilt-tripped' out of it but if you are busy and have to stay in, give your colleagues a break by avoiding fish or egg.

The same applies to leaving. If your work is done and the official time to leave is upon you, go home. Have a life. Why hang about, afraid of being the first one to leave? I always felt guilty about dashing out the door on a quiet day until I forgot something at the train station one day and had to return to my desk ten minutes later. The place was dead. Others literally wait for the first one to go and then the floodgates open. Be a trendsetter. On the other hand, if something is going down, it should be all hands on deck and you should expect to cancel your social life until it's sorted (and not necessarily get paid for the extra hours – you're putting in the effort to show your commitment, not your greed).

> **NB When it comes to lunch**, don't feel obliged to gather the waifs and strays and invite them to dine with you every day. Go with your buddies and take time out. But if you're having a bigger event for a birthday or something, invite everyone. No one likes to be the only person left out. Paranoia is a horrible thing to deal with at work. When you ask a business contact to lunch, you're picking up the tab and vice versa.

Communicating at work

Getting heard in meetings

Meetings are so tedious and often a waste of time. Why can't they just let you get on with the work? Because things need to be organised and meetings are the best way of informing everyone of developments, that's why. How should you handle yourself?

1. Always arrive on time, sober and with a bottle of water if you suffer from a dry mouth.

2. Have a notebook and pen, and all your ideas listed clearly.

3. Don't criticise your colleagues' ideas unless you have an alternative, or can justify your complaint.

4. Don't sulk if an idea of yours is rejected. Get on with it – you're all working to the same end.

5. Check your body language – folded arms, scratching or leaning back show arrogance and lack of interest.

6. Speak clearly and evenly and use examples to back up your stance. Don't raise your voice or shout, or cry, or laugh like a mad, rocking-chair old gran.

7. Be brave. If the meeting is drawing to a close and you have something to say, speak up – you could be about to save the company millions!

8. Try not to be intimidated. If you weren't worthy of being there, you wouldn't be there.

9. Make brief notes during the meeting but concentrate on following the debate, looking at visual aids and checking eye contact.

10. Immediately after the meeting, make more detailed notes and write a 'to do' list of your new aims and/or responsibilities.

Final tips on meeting etiquette for the busy:

♦ Always arrange a meeting in someone else's office (it's easier to leave, than make someone leave).

♦ Arrange meetings at odd times (11.40, rather than 11.30) – it will stop the tendency to talk for a fixed half-hour or longer.

♦ And finally, try taking a short meeting standing up – it will keep all parties focused and to the point.

Networking

Smarming and schmaltzing are seen as such an important part of the modern working life. They smooth the career path... and get you things more quickly and cheaply. I'm allergic to fake flattery, physically repelled by the thought of arse-licking... but it is important.

I would say to those like me, discriminate. Don't arse-lick *everyone*, only those you really feel deserve it. This will make them feel special, and you feel less like a scumbag.

Nepotism still exists – despicable though it is – but try and make a modern girls' network to rival the old boys' variety. You'll be much better to look at.

In reality, the best way to network is to be well-mannered and kind to everyone, for that lowly work-experience girl could one day be your boss. Forget about only networking upwards. Throw the net wide.

Managing upwards

You don't only have to look after your direct reports and clients, you also have to manage your boss so they can manage you effectively. Mutual respect is what you should be aiming for. Here's how:

◆ Be honest – say when something is wrong or inaccurate so that when you say something is good, they know that your judgment can be trusted.

◆ Don't snitch on other members of the team but keep an eye on people if you are asked to.

◆ If your boss asks you to be somewhere, be there. If they ask you to do something, do it.

◆ If you have a genuine issue, go directly and quickly to them to raise it. Don't go over their head.

♦ Remember, some bosses like bullshit, but all good bosses like good workers.

Managing downwards

Looking after a team involves diplomacy, kindness, fairness and motivation. Encourage your staff to work harder and reward them when they do. If the company can't afford pay rises, invent your own incentives like a big night out or an away-day at a spa. Avoid patronising – assume your team are as valuable and as intelligent as you, just with less experience or different strengths. And remember not everyone wants to be a leader, so don't assume they're all after your job. Most staff just want someone level-headed they can learn from. If you're having a bad day, warn them. If one of them is disappointing you, point out why and give them time to improve. Tyrants never prosper.

Disciplining the disorderly

1. Do it in private.

2. Make notes before you go in so you cannot be won over or caught off-guard.

3. Ask for a member of the human resources department to go with you if you sense a tricky situation.

4. Let the disorderly speak and answer your questions.

5. Agree the way forward. What should they change? How can they do so?

6. Set another meeting for one week/month's time to check progress.

7. Register proceedings with your boss and human resources in case things don't improve.

8. Do not bring personal grudges or judgements into the workplace.

Office politics

Basically, keep your nose clean. Office politics can quickly turn open, generous people into hideous old hags – bitching like witches does nothing for your posture. Unless you are specifically asked your opinion on something, stay out of it. Don't speculate or exaggerate – this isn't a soap opera, it's professional life. If you're hanging around the smoking-room scaring passers-by with news of fictional problems, you've got too much time on your hands. Go to the boss and ask to become fire warden for your floor.

My previous jobs at monthly magazines have had their fair share of backstabbing and meetings about nothing. It's amazing the difference being at a weekly magazine makes – we're all too busy to dislike each other, and even pull together to make the product better and the staff happier.

If you have a genuine issue, go to the person who can help with a realistic aim in mind. Be honest, fair and open-minded.

The office party

So, your working life is steady, everyone gets on OK – and then you go out after-hours and get hideously pissed. The office will never be the same again. Not only are your promotion prospects hampered by the wet T-shirt competition you instigated at midnight, but also you saw a different side to your boss when he danced to his own private beat-box. Will you ever be able to show your face again? Will he?

Pay heed to the following:

1. Don't drink too much and if there's food, remember to eat some.

2. Try to leave work frustrations in the office.

3. If pursuing a romantic liaison, think really carefully about the ramifications of making your interest public.

4. Avoid colleagues who have a camera, unless you're prepared for the results to be mailed round the office.

5. Use the opportunity to get to know others outside your immediate team. This will pay massive workplace dividends. Your goal should be broadening daily relations, not career-furthering opportunism – but it can't hurt!

6. Don't drink too much.

You'll notice that I mentioned the danger of alcohol twice. Drunkenness and decorum simply do not mix. If you have had one too many, pay heed to the advice in the following two sections.

Who to avoid at the work bash

♦ **The boss's wife:** in case you vomit on her – or even worse, bore her with your foolish ramblings while spitting Pringles in her direction.

♦ **Your assistant:** three G'n'Ts in, you'll be offering her a pay rise you can't fulfil. And if she's not to be trusted, she'll have plenty of ammunition for the morning.

♦ **The office pervert:** do not, I repeat, do not let the groper get the better of you in a weak moment. Even if he does look better through your double-vision beer goggles.

- **Your clients:** not strictly true – when you first arrive you should make them feel welcome, introduce them to key people and get them drinks and snacks. It's only if you have a few too many you should steer clear. You're not only representing yourself, you're representing your company.

- **Your partner:** don't invite loved ones if at all possible. They won't know anyone, you'll be saddled with them all night and let's face it, work people can seem weird at the best of times and if you're not in the same industry, forget it.

Who to avoid *becoming* at your work bash

- **The office pervert:** you may think you look like J-Lo on a good day, irresistible to men with a rack to die for. You're not. The tequila slammers have left you a dribbling, staggering mess with wandering hands. Only the very needy will take advantage of you.

- **The 'I love you' woman:** the dangerous cocktail of excitement, booze and no food has really got to you. You get misty-eyed telling your boss how supportive he's been, slow dance with the guy from accounts and sign everyone up for a charity fun run. There's nothing fun about running. Remember that even when lashed.

- **The amnesiac:** was it a good party? God knows. You vaguely remember getting a taxi to the venue with your department – and there's a slight recollection of praying at the porcelain temple. Get the low-down before venturing into the office the next day.

- **The dark horse:** you're normally so placid and sweet, dear. Not anymore – the mask has come off to reveal a hyperactive dancing fiend! You go, girl, let your hair down, but be prepared for mickey-taking the next day (and sore feet).

◆ **The enraged one:** booze makes you angry, you turn bright red, storm up to the managing director and take the piss out of his favourite tie. How could you? You'll have a lot of apologising to do tomorrow, young lady.

CLAIRE, 29

❝ Last year our female head of marketing got very drunk at a client conference and proceeded to molest some of her male colleagues. She was escorted back to her room by the big boss and a member of hotel staff. After ten minutes she re-emerged, this time to publicly make an explicit suggestion to a client! Fortunately(?) for her, she didn't remember anything about what had happened and therefore didn't have any qualms about showing her face in public again. Unfortunately, not all the attendees at that event were quite as forgetful. Stories spread like wildfire throughout the organisation and to this day people still snigger when she walks past. ❞

Away-days

Work trips are worse than office parties because there is a longer period of time in which you can look stupid. Pace yourself. Don't get stinking drunk on the first night and spend the rest of the away-days grimacing whenever the trays of sandwiches are passed round. And sorry to be a party pooper, but you are there to work. Be alert. Keep the drinking, dancing and late nights to a minimum (and between the hours of 8 p.m. and 1 a.m.). Don't treat it like a holiday, and don't do anything you wouldn't want known in the office. Unless you have a 'what goes on tour, stays on tour' rule like most rock bands.

Working relationships

Twenty-eight per cent of *Cosmopolitan* readers have had sex in a car park after a work Christmas party. Well, blow me! Well, you're obviously too busy blowing each other, but, er, shouldn't you be a bit more discerning? If work relationships end, they'll be embarrassment and awkwardness all round – even your colleagues will feel the pressure. Sure, sleep with your boss if you fancy him and he respects you, sex or no sex. Don't sleep with him to get a pay rise or to make the other girls in the office jealous. If you do start shagging, keep it quiet – even if he's not giving you any special treatment, your co-workers will assume there's favouritism. And whatever you do, don't be over-familiar in front of anyone. It's sick-making watching couples slobber at the best of times… but your boss? Eek! People will think it's funny and speculate on where you have sex (his desk) and what you say while you're doing it ('You're a thrusting young administrator, Ms Jones!') Fair play to them. You'd gossip too.

If you are the boss, think carefully about whom you set your sights on. It's a sad reality that women are still labelled in the sexual arena and if you shack up with a young stud on the graduate scheme, people will use the words 'toy boy' and 'outrageous'. If he's worth it, silence your critics by having a decent, respectful relationship. Keep quiet if it's a one-nighter after the office bash, or choose your men more carefully.

LYNNE, 27

❝ My current bloke and I have inspired much gossip. Offices are pretty dull places and people depend on illicit inter-colleague shagging (real or imaginary) to spice things up. If you do decide to embark on a relationship with a colleague, be prepared for lots of interest. We managed to keep a lid on our romance for a month or so – a practice I'd strongly recommend. It gives you time to work out whether you're going to work out. And remember, while your snoopy colleagues will want to know if you're doing the deed, they won't want to see evidence of it. So you'll never catch me blowing kisses over the computers. ❞

Office romances are usually a bad idea. First, you may be fooled into thinking you've got more in common than you really have just because you both happen to hate the same wally in accounts. Second, if it doesn't work out you could be left with your ex glaring at you across the office or you crying in the toilets because the bastard ditched you. If it's a messy split, your colleagues will probably feel awkward and might even take sides – not great, especially if they take pity on him instead of you. People have left jobs for far less.

Job changes

Asking for more money

This can be a nightmare. But it doesn't have to be. Employers know the going rate for a conscientious, clever girl like you and so have probably been expecting your tap on the door for quite some time. Go in there and justify your need for a salary review by explaining how your job description has now widened and you are being underpaid in the industry.

The worst that can happen is your boss says 'no', but agrees to review the situation again in a set amount of time. Bosses do know that a static salary reduces loyalty and after-hours work.

Getting promoted

Congratulations! You deserved it... now how should you reform your behaviour? First, tell everyone as soon as it's official, or the other workers may feel excluded. Don't distance yourself from people in your old team (they'll accuse you of being above your station) although, realistically, you will have less time to chat now. They might feel a little strange that their buddy can now tell them what to do. In this case, show them you find it awkward too and always ask politely when you need them to do something. Don't show favouritism. It takes six months to be fully productive in a new role, so for the time being, work is purely about work. Don't feel guilty that you've been upgraded while others – who've perhaps been at the company longer – are still floundering. The best person was given the job, and that was you. But don't rub it in. Don't strut around the office. You've only been promoted, not won a Nobel Peace Prize.

> **NB If a colleague** – or even worse a work friend – gets promoted over you, be gracious, smile and say, 'Well done.' Short of leaving, there's nothing you can do about it. And you may need that person in the future, so don't bitch.

Getting sacked

Ouch. 'Why me? Am I a dreadful person?' No, of course not, but be honest with yourself. Is your timekeeping a little lacking? Do you have an issue with authority? Employers must give employees multiple warnings before they fire them, so if you didn't pull your socks up after those, more fool you.

When you receive a warning, you should stay calm, listen to what your boss has to say, try to see their point of view and promise to improve. Treat warnings like a trip to the therapist: they help you to understand how others see you and how you could be a better person as a result. Tribunals are often an effective solution for both parties.

Of course, getting the boot could be just what you need – a sharp, firm kick up the backside to get you out of a dead-end job or away from a miserable environment. Make the most of it and start from scratch – think about what would make you happy.

If you believe you've been unfairly dismissed, however, go straight to human resources or the citizens advice bureau. Some bosses have their own agenda, or they don't like the look of their new underling. Some are even scared by younger/thinner/nicer assistants climbing up the ladder and are determined to damage the 'opposition' as soon as possible. This is not on. Complain quickly, with dignity. Older women aren't necessarily warm and sharing – some are jealous and paranoid. Maybe you'll feel the same when young dudes are waiting to take your crown, although you really should be more self-assured and kind than that.

Sacking someone

Sacking someone can be almost as distressing as being sacked if you're a nice person without Machiavellian tendencies. Before you agree to be the hangman, check the facts, know your position and understand this isn't a debate. The person has to go.

If you don't agree with the sacking, refuse to do it. Offer to give an official warning instead or say someone must do their own dirty work.

The reality of redundancy

Being made redundant is also a dreadful, helpless feeling. OK, you haven't done anything wrong, but the word 'redundant' is so damning – it literally means 'of no use'. And you've got rent to pay, a mortgage to save for. Suddenly the rug is pulled away from under your feet and you have to start again. The best advice I can give is to keep calm and try to see the bigger picture. Life does go on. I've been there and life does get easier again.

CAMILLA, 32

❝ I was made redundant unexpectedly a few years ago and embarrassed myself by crying (for "crying" also read "wailing") during the official announcement from the big boss. But looking back, it was a positive move to let the shock and anger out so quickly. I spent a few days tying up loose ends, updating my contacts book and informing everyone of my move. (Everybody was sympathetic – sadly, it's a sign of the modern age that most people have been affected by redundancy.) Then I was out – no mucking about – looking for new work, meeting up with people who could help and looking forward to the future. Others lingered around the old offices like ghosts, not quite believing their time had been and gone and using the time to moan and procrastinate. If you want time off, fine, but use it to think ahead. If you live in the past you'll have to rely on your pay-off to live, whereas I used mine to redecorate my bathroom because I refused to feel "redundant".

So long, farewell...

Leave on a good note if at all possible. Don't hand in your resignation and stagger through the one-month notice period permanently hungover, grouchy and sarcastic. Don't run around the office in a cheerleading outfit, screaming 'I'm free!' Do thank your boss (even if the relationship hasn't been great) for their help and kindness. Do ask to reduce the notice period if you think it will be unbearably long for everyone concerned – your heart won't be in the job and people may no longer trust you. Don't encourage others to follow you… at least for now. Wait till you're settled, then poach people if you can offer them more money/security/happiness. Get your stuff together when everyone else has left – no snooping for business contacts, only take yours. Don't show off about your new, fabulous job, just explain it was too good an opportunity to pass up and you'll miss everyone a lot. Even if you're lying, it will make you look gracious and make those staying behind feel secure.

Secrets of Success

◆ Remember work is important, but it's not the be all and end all. Only live through your job when everything else is bad or your career needs extra attention. Don't wake up one day and realise you've let your friends and family down in your bid to be a millionairess.

◆ Keep your CV updated as you achieve more things. Compile different CVs for different job applications

◆ Don't be pushy in interviews. No one likes a show-off, least of all a future boss who needs a team player.

◆ Try not to fidget too much in an interview. And don't smile gormlessly when answering serious questions. Keep your brain connected to your facial expressions at all times.

◆ If you haven't heard anything two weeks after an interview, do call or e-mail to see if a decision has been made. It is impolite of the employers to keep you dangling like this.

◆ Don't feel bitter at being an assistant or secretary – even if you know you could do a job better than your boss. Everyone has to start somewhere and I believe you can never truly ask someone to do something if you're not prepared to do it yourself. It's all good training.

◆ Get adopted. Find a mentor, pick their brains and ask them to show you the ropes. You'll learn and they'll feel flattered. Repay the compliment with an up-and-coming 'you' one day. Never steal your mentor's contacts or information. Return their good will with good grace.

◆ You can't love all the people all the time. Avoid colleagues who get your back up – you don't need a public brawl. Just understand people do things differently... and you do it better anyway. Remember, people only pick on others if they are jealous or unhappy in their own lives.

◆ Treat your assistants well. Don't shower them with gifts like an overenthusiastic sugar daddy, but be thoughtful. Give them things you know they'd like, take them with you to events you know they'd benefit from and take time out to train them.

◆ ...But don't let them take the piss. They are there to *assist* you, after all. They should be prepared to do the dogsbody stuff, and even get lunch for you if you're in back-to-back meetings. As long as you ask politely.

◆ Don't take the mickey with expenses. You can claim work costs and that's it. Your boss may sign your expense forms and put them through for ease, but it's undoubtedly a black mark against your name – and is it really worth the stress of seeing whether you can charge the company for the boozy lunch with a friend?

◆ Don't be too honest at your leaving party and never slag off your boss, colleagues or the company. Fate has a funny way of bringing people back together again.

Chapter Five

Communication
conundrums

How do you send the right message to people? With so many devices to keep us connected 24/7, staying in touch has never been easier but we need a new set of manners to keep us in touch...

Letters

How to write a letter people want to read

Try not to analyse your writing style or worry too much about spelling and punctuation. As long as a letter's legible and well meant, friends won't really care about the details. That being said, if it's important or official correspondence, then dictionaries (electronic or otherwise) are there for a reason and can do much to help your message be taken seriously.

If it's a personal note, write clearly on clean paper. Don't waste time if your hand aches after years on a computer – get straight down to events, people and your feelings since you last met. Include photographs if you have some the recipient would like. Ask more than just how they are – remember worries and changes and write concerning their developments. Sign off however you wish, with genuine affection and lots of kisses.

When writing is write

◆ Formal invitations – if you post an invite, guests will automatically assume 'a bit of a do'. Include time, place and dress code and ask for details of allergies or vegetarians. State the names of the people you're inviting clearly, otherwise people may show up to elegant soirées with their kids in tow.

◆ Thank-you letters show thought because they take time and effort. Handwritten ones are lovely to receive and a rare treat these days. Make the effort and set aside an afternoon after your birthday or Christmas or a party to write them. Refer to the gift or good deed directly, give a few lines of news and ask how the person is before signing off with another thank-you and best wishes. Your effort will be appreciated.

◆ Birthday cards must be sent – an e-mail, fax or phone call isn't the same. Even if you are seeing the person on their special day, a card will give them something to keep, laugh at and remember. Everyone loves it when a little effort is made.

◆ When someone close to you loses a loved one, it is kind and appropriate to send an 'in sympathy' card. Express your regret and tell a personal anecdote about the deceased. Keep it brief and sincere and don't talk about yourself.

◆ Posting a 'get well soon' card is a good way of cheering up the sick and immobile when they're trapped at home with nothing but daytime television and a tin of soup for company.

◆ Although it's time-consuming to write to a friend with all your news and gossip, sometimes it's nice to sit with your thoughts on a spare rainy afternoon and waffle on and on. You might not be in the mood to chat on the telephone and you could call at the wrong time for your friend. Receiving a letter is a luxury and it can be enjoyed with a cup of tea at the right time.

CATHERINE, 29

❛ It really annoys me when people don't properly thank you for birthday or wedding presents. If they say it, then it should be a very clear thank-you, not an almost embarrassed quiet thank-you! It is also nice, especially for weddings, to have a written thank-you within a few weeks, not four or five months later. It's one thing that really annoys me – even if the recipient is grateful, they must communicate this. We can't read people's minds! I don't want to give names, but after one wedding, I didn't get a letter until three months after the big day.

Another annoyance are those shop-bought, pre-written notelets where you just have to fill in the names of the people – very slapdash and unworthy of a proper thank-you unless a decent-sized paragraph is written in addition! 🟡

We'll mail again...
Contacting people after a long time has passed is always difficult, but sometimes it's worth making the effort. Chances are, they'll be missing you too.

One of the most difficult types of letter to write is to an old friend you've fallen out with. You've been horrible to them, they've been rude about you and before you know it a year – and a lot of bad blood – has passed between you. With time, things usually cool down and you invariably realise you need this person in your life, so try sending a birthday or Christmas card with a letter saying how much you miss them and that life is too short to make such a mistake. Nine times out of ten they'll contact you in return – writing gives someone time to think about their response – and you've a good chance of becoming buddies again. The power of the pen, ay!

So never think it's too late, or you're both too different, or they'll have forgotten you. Even if they have, it will be a nice trip down memory lane to be reminded. Search for details through mutual friends, Internet sites like Friends Reunited, or try writing to their last known address... their mum could still be there. Don't get too heavy, nosy or possessive. Fill them in on your latest events and remind them of the good old days. Give them your e-mail address and phone number – options are good when you haven't spoken to someone for a long time.

I remember you...
Keeping a record of important events will win many
Brownie points with your friends and family. Birthdays,
anniversaries, exam-passing, etc. should all be celebrated
with a congratulatory card.

Some people are naturally wonderful and organised –
they keep an emergency supply of cards in their bedside
cabinet and a packet of stamps in their purse. Others need
help. Here are some tips:

1. When you get next year's diary at the end of December,
   transfer all dates immediately. You won't remember them
   in your head.

2. Admit forgetfulness (or pretend you've lost your address
   book). On a quiet day at work, e-mail all loved ones
   asking for their addresses, birthdays and special events. It
   will only take them a second to reply. Then compile a list
   and attach it immediately to your diary, or copy it out
   neatly.

3. Borrow your mother's and/or close friend's organised
   planner and steal their hard work.

4. Ask friends to text you their birthdays and set them
   straight on to your phone's reminder alarm – you may
   not get the card out in time, but at least you can ring or
   text first thing in the morning with your good wishes.

5. If you've got the cash, hire a personal organiser. They are
   more and more common and can be found in phone
   directories. Not only do they buy and send cards and
   presents on your behalf, they also take charge of bills,
   expenses and household chores.

> **NB Apart from your parents**, you are under no obligation to send wedding anniversary cards to people after their first year of marriage, until the big ones: 10, 25, 50, etc. But it's always nice to know your special day has been remembered – and if you played a part in someone's wedding, think about making an effort or at least ring them.

When writing is wrong

◆ Never end a relationship via a letter. That whole 'Dear John' thing is very cold. A modern girl takes the higher ground and dumps her man face to face... Ignore the begging and weeping and do what you have to do.

◆ Don't announce a redundancy or sacking over the phone or by letter. You need to react to the person as you give the bad news and offer advice, reassurance and criticism. Soften the edges with a personal approach.

◆ Try to break good tidings to those close to you in person. Telling your family you're engaged or expecting a baby is too good an opportunity to waste – you'll want to see their faces and have the chance to celebrate together.

◆ Likewise, if you have really bad news, you need be able to comfort the person immediately. It's hard to see the tears, but you need to be there for those moments and to think about the future.

◆ If you're cancelling a date, it's polite to call the person to rearrange a time and place. Doing this via e-mail can seem a bit inconsiderate (and even as though you've had a better offer and want to clear your diary sharpish without explanation).

Opening other people's mail

Everyone needs privacy. This should be obvious. You shouldn't even have to establish this ground rule with those you live or work with, but occasionally it's worthwhile.

And don't assume that once you are in a relationship you each forfeit the right to keep your post secret. I'm not just talking the emotional stuff, but also business-related correspondence. If you need to know what's going on with each other's finances, get a joint account or have a kitty for general household expenses.

If mail does arrive for another person and you really can't resist it, ring and offer to open it for them while they are on the phone. Make it sound so exciting that they can't wait to find out what it is either. Give postmark info and any other clues. If they still say no, respect that. Don't boil the kettle for a cup of tea and a quick steam. That's a bit too nosy.

If someone asks you to check their mail, open it and read briefly. If they need to hear more, they will ask. It's normally just to put *their* mind at rest and shouldn't be taken as a mandate to continue.

NATALIE, 29

❝ My husband and I went through a phase of opening each other's mail when we first got married. Then he opened a letter addressed to me and found out about a Christmas present and I threw away his treasured football club fanzine thinking it was junk mail, and we both decided it wasn't a good idea. ❞

Electronic etiquette

Is e-mail the best bloody invention in the world or what? It saves time, effort… and making those dreaded calls to a client. But are we too reliant on our little mouse? Some modern girls are so PC-friendly they now find it impossible to lift a phone receiver and actually *talk* to someone. Tut, tut, modern girl.

E-mail pros
All the information sent to you is stored for your records, you can keep a back-up of what has been sent/said, you can copy others, you can 'blind' copy others…

E-mail cons
Your tone can be misinterpreted, your computer can break (whole offices can come to a standstill when the e-mail does), you stop talking to people a few feet away and it allows easy backstabbing in the office.

How to write an e-mail

1. E-mails save time, so don't write one like a letter, with date, address and formal greetings. Be brief and to the point.

2. Reference e-mails clearly in the subject box. Update the title if the same e-mail is being sent to and fro, or forwarded to someone else.

3. Capitals can be rude out of context – you may mean to emphasise a point, others will think you're angry, shouting or impatient. Only go upper case one word at a time for dramatic impact.

4. Don't try to be too funny or sarcastic – it's impossible in type.

5. Try not to write more than one screen of text. Most people read e-mails at work and will only be able to skim-read quickly.

6. Don't forward annoying files or silly chain letters. They don't work or, if you can get them open, you always wonder why you bothered. If you can't e-mail a personal message, don't bother. Circulars are the bane of a busy person's life.

7. Don't get angry if you don't receive a reply straightaway. Everyone has their own agenda. If it is incredibly urgent, pick up the phone and talk.

8. Don't try and defuse a worrying subject via e-mail. Be brave and go and see the troublemaker face to face or call them. Things will be solved sooner, and off the record if necessary, and you won't have nightmares about what's waiting in your inbox the next morning.

9. Don't blind copy unless necessary. If people think they are having a private discussion, it's unfair for a third person to be in on the act. Also, check the e-mail address carefully before you send. Be vigilant.

10. Don't write anything on e-mail you wouldn't want your boss to find out. Most companies do monitor them and the geeks in the basement are often required to store them for a set period. Sometimes company computers are fixed to pick up on swear words and anti-firm banter, so keep it clean.

Keep me hanging on

Using the telephone should be such a simple thing – so why does it fill so many of us with terror? The answer is simple I'm afraid: because it requires paying attention, listening and for you to engage actively with the caller, even when you don't feel like it. It's quite common in these quick-fix, hectic times to disregard calling people – for fear of disrupting their routine, or in case you get caught up in a long session. Yet the telephone isn't the enemy of those without time or patience. It should still be cherished as an extremely personal way of communicating, especially over long distances.

A good telephone manner is an essential skill in the modern world, whether responding to a prospective date, persuading a client or handling a nosy mother. Never assume the person on the other end of the line knows who you are, so be prepared to introduce yourself and give your reason for calling, always speak clearly and try not to use the phone as a shield for when you should really do something face to face but are simply too scared.

Sometimes it is OK to be a little selfish and only phone for a reason: maybe when arranging a time to meet, cancelling an engagement or saying 'happy birthday'. General chitchats can still be fun, but arrange a time beforehand via e-mail, or check as soon as you get through that now is a convenient time.

Don't be afraid to bring the conversation to an end after a set time if you have other things to do. Try saying 'Hiya, I've only got 15 minutes, but I'm desperate to hear all about your holiday. Was it amazing?' This places a subject and time limit. Busy, modern girls prefer to have set boundaries than listen to an abundance of waffling about nothing throughout their favourite soap opera or endure long silences from someone who has nothing to say but feels they should stay on the line for an hour because it's off-peak rates.

Don't speak

A phone call before or after a certain time can instil fear into the weak-hearted, so think before you lift the receiver...

1. Before 8 a.m.

2. After 10 p.m.

3. To dial a house where you know someone is poorly or elderly.

4. To dial a business outside working hours – you'll be frustrated by the security guard and vice versa.

5. With mobiles, if someone is abroad – even though you are making the call, *they* can be charged an exorbitant connection fee.

How to leave messages

Many people are scared by the 'bleep bleep' of an answering machine and instantly hang up rather than leave a dithering blur of 'erms' for their friend, or worse still client, to return to. No need. Remember the following:

- Everyone sounds strange on answering machines, so don't worry about your tone or accent.

- No one will analyse what you say, just wait for the basic message.

- Keep it brief – you don't want to use up too much tape and be stopped mid-sentence.

- Keep to the point. If you panic and can't think of what to say, stick with your name, the time you called and your number.

- If it's someone you know well, don't worry about being formal – talk to them as you would in person.

- Don't leave a rude or personal message on an answering machine. Someone else might get to it before your confidante. Likewise, don't say 'Hiya. Just calling to hear the gossip from your hot date,' in case your friend's mum pops in to do the cleaning and listens in.

- Messages do get lost or garbled, so if you haven't heard back in 24 hours, call again. It won't seem needy.

- Don't leave ten messages in the space of an hour – give the person time to check their machine.

- Don't lie if you're somewhere you shouldn't be in case a train announcement goes off or the recipient of your call checks the number you were dialling from.

- Leaving messages can be good if you want to remind someone of something but don't want to get caught up chatting. Leave a message while they are at work, etc.

- Practise etiquette by leaving messages for yourself. You can fine-tune your speech *and* remind yourself to bring in your gym kit the next day.

- While we're talking about message etiquette, *always* note down your own messages carefully and pass them on if necessary. If you're actually on the phone to someone and haven't got a pen handy, be upfront and ask the caller to ring back later.

Sending out the right message

Recording your own answerphone message is a chance to give all and sundry a glimpse into your psyche. A brief, professional 'I'm not available to take your call at the moment. Please leave your name and number and I'll get back to you when I can' is always polite. A cheeky, friendly message ('Howdy, cowboys! Leave your number and I'll get back to you if I can be bothered') may amuse your friends the first time they hear it, but upset your accountant. A song can make a statement but can quickly become annoying and a waste of a modern girl's valuable seconds. Never swear, burp or make a political statement. Don't leave your address or other phone numbers.

Mobiles

Using a cell-phone is no longer unique or a novelty – so there's nothing to show off about. Remember that you and your life are not the centre of the universe, therefore not everyone wants to hear your conversation. If you're in a crowded place, go outside or somewhere more private, and if you have to shout, i.e. on the train, shut up and call back at a more appropriate time. You may think your plans for tonight deserve an audience. Tired commuters won't.

In a similar vein, pay attention to both the volume and sound of your ring-tone – some are far more irritating than others – and maybe do a test with some honest friends if you really can't tell what might be aurally offensive.

Many people get flustered when it comes to the rules on answering someone else's mobile. There is a simple rule: what would you would be able to do if left alone in that person's house when the landline started ringing? If you're not confident you'd be able to pick up the receiver, then apply the same logic. Besides, if they were expecting an urgent call they would have taken their mobile with them. Also, one of the great things about mobiles is that they leave a record of who called, and often messages, so there's no need to be unduly worried.

> **RALPH**, 28 (an honorary girl when it comes to phone etiquette)
>
> ❝ All phones should be switched to 'silent' in restaurants, cafés, bars, cinemas, etc., and shouldn't be answered whilst you are dining/drinking, etc., with friends, especially if there are only two of you (the larger the group, the less of a problem, assuming you are not speaking with somebody at the time your phone rings). Surely it is rude to ignore a friend who you have arranged to meet whilst you chat to someone else, leaving them to sit and twiddle their thumbs. Your whole attention should be directed to the person with whom you are spending time. The reverse is also true: the caller deserves your full attention. Nothing in life (apart from water) is more important than your relationships. You wouldn't do it with an important client, would you? Likewise with text messages. Yet we all seem to be programmed like Pavlovian dogs to answer the phone without question... ❞

Let's talk about text

Texting can be quick, cheap and flirty – and can be ignored until you are ready to respond, which is the greatest thing of all. The one rule is: don't become a text bore. It's rude to text people when you're with others. Especially on a date (unless you are hoping to get rid of your beau). If you receive a text, do check it immediately by all means – and if it's urgent, respond. If it's just a random, gossipy message, ignore it until you're on your own... it will be a useful distraction when your companion goes to the loo. Again, be considerate when texting furiously – it can be irritating in certain environments.

Fax of life

Remember faxes? Occasionally, you will still be required to send one, so always check how the fax machines work and where they are when you move to a new firm. If someone asks for a fax, don't bark 'It's an e-mail or nothing, you dinosaur.' Some people do prefer faxes – and the piles of filing that come with them.

If possible, when sending a fax use headed paper and print the number of sheets sent and the name it is destined for clearly. Faxes are more formal than e-mails or memos – you must include the date, your contact details and sign off appropriately, be it with a 'yours faithfully' (if you've never met the person), 'yours sincerely' (if you're acquaintances) or 'best regards' (if you've met a few times). Hover about to check that it goes through OK or follow up with a phone call to make sure it reached its destination.

Secrets of Success

♦ 'Listen more than you talk' may be the rule when talking face to face with someone but when you e-mail, phone or write, you must set the pace and deliver news. There is nothing worse than a silent caller or an e-mail filled with questions instead of lively anecdotes.

◆ Always start a letter, e-mail or phone call with a sincere 'How are you?' Manners cost nothing, remember.

◆ Beware of speakerphone. You don't want your boyfriend's colleagues to have a laugh at your expense.

◆ If viruses are going around your e-mail group or firm, warn those on your address list as soon as possible.

◆ E-mails can be as sentimental as letters. Print the special ones and keep them in case your server gets wiped.

◆ If you can contact someone on a landline, do so. Mobiles can be inconvenient and bad reception can leave you screaming.

◆ Avoid phoning or e-mailing when you are drunk or angry. You'll only regret it... Sober up or count to ten and then make contact.

◆ Every modern girl should keep an up-to-date address book, stamps and writing paper to drop someone a line when they need to hear from her. Letters are old- fashioned, but always a wonderful surprise.

◆ Stalking via phone or e-mail is still stalking.

◆ Check your messages regularly and return calls as soon as possible. The same applies to e-mails.

◆ Faxing or mailing correspondence forces you to be more careful about what you are writing, so address any formal or legal matters this way.

◆ When dating new people, give out your mobile number, not your home number.

◆ When using your mobile, use the earpiece device with caution – people may think you're mad or talking to yourself. If you keep chitchat brief, your brain won't fry.

◆ If your phone rings during a face-to-face conversation with another person, ignore it (especially if you're talking to your boss) or switch it off completely and let the caller leave a message. Locate the 'silence' mode too.

◆ If someone hasn't responded to your letter/e-mail or call after three attempts, they don't want to. Drop it.

◆ Try to avoid calling expensive phone lines: they can't really predict your future, find you love or give you a party atmosphere down the line ... just a huge bill.

Chapter Six

Food for thought

FOOD, GLORIOUS FOOD – one of life's greatest pleasures and by far the best accessory with which to navigate a social situation. If in doubt, introduce food and wine and most rational people will start to relax, or at the very least have something to occupy their time with. So, if us modern girls love nothing more than a good grub-fest, which rules should be observed while we're doing so?

Restaurants

All of us have felt intimidated at some time or another when going out for a meal. Whether faced with a particularly rude waiter, appalling food or an unfathomable menu, an uncertainty about the correct way to behave is not unusual.

My first piece of advice is always pick a venue that you and your fellow diner(s) will feel comfortable with. I'm not just talking about dress code and everyone's bank balance – it's also worth ensuring that everyone in your party can be accommodated too. For example, check ahead about vegetarian options, high chairs for kids, dishes for those who may have certain allergies or even the proximity of car parking if anyone in your party has mobility problems.

An important truth to remember is that relaxed, or cheaper, environments will not automatically mean that the food and service will be towards the lower end of the scale, far from it. Similarly, often the snobbiest establishments really have no excuse for behaving in such a way. That being said, if you want to do something with a bit of style or blow the bank, don't hesitate – your money is as good as anyone else's. Just get out there and act confidently. Ask those you trust for recommendations before making your decision.

How to book a table

Remember, you are the customer. Don't be put off by a snooty voice even when you call the hottest restaurant in town to make a reservation. They need you more than you need them.

How can you be sure to get a good table?

◆ Book at least two weeks in advance.

◆ Keep your group to under eight people.

◆ Think about dining before 8.30 p.m. or after 10.30 p.m.

◆ Mention it's a special occasion.

♦ Pretend to be a celebrity, a journalist or in public relations. It sounds silly, but if desperate, pretend to be your own PA too – always impressive.

♦ Offer to go in smoking or non-smoking, i.e. be flexible, if that's OK with everyone in your party.

♦ Avoid Thursday, Friday and Saturday.

♦ Ask for the menu to be faxed or e-mailed to you – this way you can check out prices and dishes before making your decision.

NB If you can't get a dinner reservation for love or money, 'do a Californian' and meet friends at the restaurant just for cocktails – that way you get to check it out, meet the maître'd and say you've been anyway. You can also ask them to put you down on the cancellation list while you're drinking. Your never know! Another Los Angeleno trick is to go out for a standard dinner and then move on to the hip eatery for dessert and liqueurs after 10 p.m. It's cool to round off an evening in a nice place.

Restaurant rituals

Once you've entered a restaurant, certain unwritten rules come into play. You should be made welcome by the staff and they should offer to take your coat from you – without you having to provide any sort of prompt. If you haven't pre-booked, then you cannot be too polite in asking if there are any spare tables. Don't argue if they say no – although a room can look empty, they may well have a number of timed reservations still to fulfil.

When you are taken to your table, don't bag a seat in the best spot before everyone has gathered round. If you are first in, move round to make it easier for everyone else. Even if it means you're stuck in social Siberia with the dullest couple on Earth, you can sit smugly knowing you're well mannered.

Remember to respect other diners. Turn down (or preferably turn off) mobile phones and pay attention to the noise level of your surroundings generally. Try not to stare at others – difficult I know, but that intimate couple in the corner may well be having a final meal to salvage their relationship and really don't need you earwigging. Nevertheless, restaurants are public environments and you are perfectly entitled to have fun and laugh, so don't be intimidated into total silence.

Ordering

Menus are there to act as a guide. If you're not sure what an ingredient is or what a certain concoction will taste like, ask the waiter. He may even get the chef out to explain. The restaurant should also advise you of any specials before you make your choice. If the menu is in another language and your schoolgirl vocabulary doesn't get you far, it's perfectly fine to ask for a translation. Chances are, if they had a menu in your native tongue, they would have given it to you when you sat down.

Only call the waiter to start placing your order when everyone is ready. Eating out is a treat and people don't like to be rushed in making their choices. Shutting your menu is the international code for 'I'm ready to order', so do that.

Always order something. There's nothing more annoying that going out for dinner or sharing a takeaway with someone who self-righteously announces, 'I'm not hungry, I'll just have a taste of yours.' No, you bloody won't... Order your own meal, sweetheart! All too often people turn up their nose (and it's women 99 per cent of the time), then wolf it all down when no one is looking. This isn't fair on the honest hungry folk.

In all things, the number one rule is: if in doubt, ask. Feel free to change a few ingredients to suit yourself – just don't do the whole Meg Ryan thing and give the waiter a list of requests, as you'll look super-fussy. If you have any allergies, though, now is the time to check that everything will suit you.

It's not terribly good manners to order a starter when everyone else wants to go straight into their main course. They'll all have to stare at your plate like orphans at a sweet-shop window. If you're starving, order a side salad to accompany your dinner instead, or ask the others to come in with you on an appetiser platter.

If you're really not hungry, try combining two starters instead of a starter and main course. Restaurants are fine about this, especially if the rest of the table are dining normally. However you should never eat two main courses – that's just greedy. Also limit your side orders… no one needs four or five extras. Your eyes are bigger than your belly.

If you've ordered some fussy food and are not quite sure how to approach it, ask. Most waiters will help the genuinely distressed.

Try to leave 20 minutes between each course to let your dinner go down, sober up and make room for dessert. Unless the restaurant has previously advised of a mandatory departure time, you are quite within your etiquette rights to sit back and relax.

How to fill your face without embarrassment
Your food is on its way so it's time to set some ground rules before it arrives. Whether taking tea at the Ritz or

munching fish 'n' chips, certain levels of decorum should be observed at all times. This has nothing to do with being posh or ladylike and everything to do with not putting those around you off their food.

Although the advice on the following pages is about restaurant etiquette, many of the tips are equally appropriate when you are invited to someone's home, or indeed, when you're the hostess. Wherever you are:

◆ Don't talk with your mouth full.

◆ Don't spit something out or make 'urgh' sounds if you don't like it. Be discreet.

◆ Don't take food off others' plates unless they've said you can/encouraged you to try something.

◆ Don't lick your fingers.

◆ Don't play with – or brush - your hair at the dinner table.

LOUISE, 24

6 How to behave in restaurants – indeed, any public situation involving food? Don't eat with your mouth open. I know your mother probably told you this when you were growing up, but you'd be surprised how many adults still do. And it's repulsive to all who dine with you. I can only assume such offenders don't know they're doing it, so ask a friend to tell you the truth. 9

Utensils and extras

Your napkin should be laid across your lap before you start eating anything. Dab your mouth with it rather than rub it with theatrical vigour. If you or your dining partner spill something, it is permissible to use your napkin to mop up the mess, but call a waiter over to rescue the tablecloth asap.

Many people panic about using the wrong knife or fork. It's simple. If you have two, three or four sets of cutlery lined up in front of you, start from the outside and work your way in with each course. The knives and forks will be positioned on the correct side. Think smaller for starter, bigger for main. Never lick or eat off your knife. If required, ask for a spoon to use during your main course rather than use your dessert one.

Your bread plate is to your left and should be cleared when your dessert arrives to make more room on the table. The bread plate is for bread and butter, not random items. It is not a sampling plate for you to pass around the table with tit-bits on.

Your wine (smaller one) and water glasses are to your right. If you are bringing a cocktail or aperitif to the table, place them to your left to save overcrowding. Only thank the waiters every other time they fill your glass – every time can interrupt the flow of conversation. Try to drink as much water as wine. You'll be thankful in the morning... You drink far more than you realise when your glass is being constantly refilled. Remember that many coffees/desserts have alcohol in them too. Drink with caution and never drink and drive.

Chopsticks can be tricky little beggars. Practise at home and it does get easier. When out, always try at first. If after a few minutes you're not getting anywhere and your stomach is rumbling, go for the fork and spoon option. At least you tried. The same goes for eating with one hand in traditional Indian restaurants.

When you eat in public, you must also be aware that quirks that your nearest and dearest find charming can turn the stomachs of strangers. My husband eats with such speed it becomes embarrassing when trying to enjoy a leisurely lunch with friends. They feel forced to rush, get indigestion, can't manage dessert... and we're in and out of the place before we know it. So he's learnt to leave his pig-truffling ways at home (even if it means having a snack before we leave the house to abate his hunger). In fact having a snack a few hours before you meet for food is often a good idea. Starve yourself all day and you will descend on the bread-basket like a vulture and scare the waitress. It's often nice to enjoy an aperitif before going straight in to dine, so don't make yourself feel faint with anticipation for a slap-up meal.

Getting started

If bread is already placed on a plate beside you before the starters have arrived, ask others if they mind you getting underway. Use the butter knife to cut the butter and place it on the side of your plate. Offer the butter dish to the person next to you. Never cut a roll with your knife – use your hands. If a waiter or waitress comes round with the bread-basket, point out which roll you would like and allow them to put it on your plate. Don't put your hands in the basket unless they say you can. It's OK to take bread when they ask you again, but don't continue once the main course has arrived, unless you are eating mussels. If the bread is stale, complain. Even though it's 'free', it should still be tasty. I often remember a restaurant by its bread-basket.

When are you allowed to start eating? If your starter or main meal is cold, you should wait until everyone has their meal in front of them before you begin. If you have a hot dish, the stragglers waiting should urge you to start in case your meal gets lukewarm. Never just start eating without consideration – especially if you are guests in someone's home and the cook hasn't sat down yet (unless they say you can).

NB Some of your dinner companions may feel compelled to say grace before eating. If so, treat this wish with respect and sit quietly while they say their piece. Don't grumble, 'Codswallop, I'm starving,' and ask your prayer buddy to pass the bread and wine.

Tricky food

It may taste great, but you could get into a terrible mess just getting it onto a fork. The following should be avoided on first dates, at business lunches and when meeting future in-laws for the first time:

- **Fondue:** tasty but can feel too intimate and porn-star seventies for sensible dining in a restaurant. And what if you don't like cheese?

- **Spaghetti and tagliatelle:** you'll get more on your chin than in your gob and you'll be too busy planning how to eat it to partake in intelligent conversation.

- **Crab and lobster:** anything involving eyeballs and a finger-dipping bowl can't be good.

- **Garlic:** only decent if you all partake, otherwise they'll be no snogging or gossiping for you, young lady.

- **Fajitas:** for friends only. Some people don't like sharing food and using their hands. Fair enough.

◆ **Hot and spicy curries:** if they stain the tablecloth that colour, what are they doing to your stomach? Delicious but smelly, and more likely than anything else to give you 'Delhi belly'.

Your fellow diners

I've already mentioned mobile phones, but equally important is resisting smoking at the table before asking your companions' permission, until the main course plates have been cleared or until the waiter has said it is OK to do so. There's nothing more disgusting than a waft of smoke ruining your last few mouthfuls. If it's a non-smoking restaurant or table, go outside. Whatever the weather.

Trips to the loo should be controlled where possible. Go more than twice during a meal and fellow diners will assume you are incontinent, abusing illegal substances or vain. Don't go to the ladies' room while you are mid-chomp. Wait until the plates have been cleared between courses. Never force anyone to go with you, but tell the girls where you're going in case they don't know the way, need to ask you something or want to borrow a lipstick/tampon/headache tablet.

If a paltry dinner's still left a hole the size of the Grand Canyon in your belly, suggest sharing a cheese platter or stock up on after-dinner mints and have a creamy drink. (If you're still starving when you get home, avoid heavy food and go for a bowl of cereal or some toast.)

The staff

How do you politely catch the eye of your waiter or waitress? First, be patient. The whole charm of 'catching someone's eye' is its subtlety, so don't be angry if it doesn't work on your first few attempts. And remember, many waiters are 'resting' actors and models, so are used to being stared at – they'll think you're just another fan. In such cases, try lifting your eyebrows. If after a fifth attempt, you're still being ignored, move your chair slightly away from the table and say 'Excuse me' when they pass within a few feet. Never use physical force and never shout 'Oi!' If you've been waiting to get your bill for over 30 minutes, stand up and put your coat on. They'll be over in a flash.

Plates should not be cleared until the last person at the table has put their knife and fork down together. It is bad form for the staff to start shuffling about while you are trying to eat and chat. It is not rude to ask them to wait and come back in ten minutes or so.

Complaining about bad service is your right but should be done quietly and politely. Some people prefer to show their dissatisfaction by leaving a measly tip (or no tip at all), but that could be misconstrued as thriftiness. If you have a genuine complaint (the food is cold, service slow, order wrong), explain that you have been patient but you are extremely disappointed. Decide what you want to get out of this – an apology, drinks on the house, a free meal – and ask for it. After remaining pleasant, if you find the restaurant unapologetic and unwilling to compensate you, warn them you will take this up with the local newspaper or health authority. See Chapter 10 for more advice in this area.

Paying the bill

If you *invited* friends to a restaurant of your choice, you should pick up the tab. If you *suggested* a new/favourite eatery, you should split the bill. Generally speaking, it should be split equally. It looks so petty and mean when friends fight over who had a coffee and who didn't. If you're a bit tight for cash and have been drinking water all night while your friends have been quaffing champagne, bring this up politely, explain the situation and ask to be removed from the drinks charge.

Bills should not be split regarding who is richer or poorer – if you can't afford to dine somewhere, suggest a different place or stay at home. Good friends will understand and change location. Neither should you feel obliged to pay for a friend who is moaning about their lowly income, even if you've just got a pay rise. If you do, you're kind, but there should be no pressure.

If you have a stingy friend who regularly throws in too little, don't be afraid to announce to the table there's not enough cash. Remind everyone they have to put in extra for a tip and give the tightwad an excuse to add something. Some real meanies will ignore your plight and stare off into the distance while you scrabble around for the extras, but at least you tried.

Tipping rules:

0% if your food has been cold, late, wrong and the staff have been rude

10% for reasonable service

15% for good service

20% for excellent food, advice, facilities and service

After you've paid the bill, don't lounge around like you own the table. A restaurant is a business. If you wish to hold on to your seat, you should continue to order drinks, etc. You should be allowed 30–45 minutes for every round of drinks you order.

Dining alone

A final restaurant-specific word about dining alone: this is perfectly normal and acceptable behaviour. If circumstances, or choice, have dictated that you are on your own, do not settle for anything other than welcoming treatment from establishments and their staff. You do not automatically deserve the worst table and staff should treat you no differently from a group. It's also perfectly fine to take along a good book for company between courses.

> **TANYA, 31**
>
> ❝ I enjoy eating alone and love trying out new restaurants. When I first started doing this, I pretended I was a food critic and took along a notepad and pen, which I left on the table in clear view. It gave me courage to have an apparent purpose and had the added benefit of ensuring I got fantastic service. I soon realised, however, that this is the 21st century and we should be able to tolerate a single person sitting alone. Now, I just go where I like and eat at whatever time suits me. It can be fun, too – I get to chat more easily to other diners and staff. It's certainly no longer intimidating. ❞

Visiting for dinner

We've tackled restaurants, but often a far greater minefield comes when someone invites us into their home. Obviously there is minimal opportunity here to choose what food we receive and opportunities to complain are extremely limited. So, make sure you know in advance what sort of occasion you are going to and ensure that any dietary requests have been made well up front. Offer to take a dish with you and always bring a token of your gratitude – some wine, chocolates or flowers. Lastly, it's absolutely vital to give compliments about aspects of the meal, setting and hospitality. You won't be leaving a tip, so you need to make your appreciation felt.

Restaurant etiquette still applies in all areas of dining – just because you have known the host all your life does not mean you can leave the table for 15 minutes to make a phone call or exhale cigarette smoke everywhere.

In fact, table manners still apply in houses, at weddings and during that quick sandwich in the park with a friend.

> **NB If you're invited to a dinner party**, you should RSVP in good time without prompting. There is nothing worse than a 'maybe'. It leaves the host feeling unwanted or unprepared. If you can't make it or don't fancy it, say so asap. Do not put off your reply in case of a better offer. That is deplorable.

When you've eaten too much...

If you feel like an overstuffed turkey at Christmas, avoid fizzy drinks and sip water instead. Strong coffee can act as a diuretic. Ignore the offer of *petits fours* and munch on an indigestion or antacid tablet instead. During the day, fight the urge to take to the sofa for a nap and go for an invigorating walk instead. Undo your trousers if possible.

When you've eaten too little...

We all have different metabolisms, so don't feel guilty if a friend or family has cooked for you and you still feel hungry. Compliment the chef profusely and hopefully you'll be offered the leftovers. Take chocolates with you and offer them round.

A good host should serve adequate food and then, a few hours after dinner, suggest drinks and snacks. If your host is lacking in etiquette, don't groan, 'I'm dying of starvation' – a bad or stingy host won't care – just say your goodbyes and stop off at the kebab house on the way home. Tasty.

MEL, 31

❝ I went to a wedding in Wales where the wine had definitely not been flowing and we'd had to wait ages for the waiter to bring another bottle to the table, which he eventually did with the cheese course. A plate of about four or five cheeses was put in front of me. I vaguely thought it was quite generous compared to the rest of the wedding meal, helped myself to a biscuit and some butter, started eating some cheese and carried on my conversation. About five minutes later a fellow guest says, "Er, can we have some cheese?" I look up and realise I've eaten about a third of the cheese which was meant for 12 people! ❞

Think while you drink

Italians wouldn't dream of indulging in a plate of pasta without a good wine to accompany it and in Australia you get offered a 'midi' of beer with breakfast. But if you're really not a big drinker, don't succumb to peer pressure. It's really not cool or clever to get pissed (but a helluva lotta fun to get merry). Don't get to the vomiting stage if you can help it. So what should you drink? And when?

Before midday

The only booze you should be perusing at this time of day is champagne (or its weaker sister, Buck's fizz) or vodka in the form of a Bloody Mary (the tomato and lemon juice makes this cocktail taste healthier than it really is). No hard liquor. Whiskeys and bourbons are out. As is anything drunk from a can – beer breath is not appropriate before lunch.

NB Serious drinkers swear by 'hair of the dog.' It's a myth. If you've got a hangover (or are still drunk by dawn if it was a really big night), you should avoid all stimulants and concentrate on rehydration and repair. Water, water, water and orange juice, I'm afraid. Avoiding coffee and tea is a good move too.

Afternoon

Drinking too much at lunch can spell professional disaster for the lily-livered lightweight. Stick with wine and equal parts water if you don't want to appear rude, or if you fancy a few. Without food, polite 'p.m.' drinks are Pimms and lemonade, G'n'Ts, Bellinis and martinis. Think fruity and frothy.

Pre-dinner

Champagne is always darling while you're getting ready for a big night out or chilling out after a stressful day. If it's hot, down a few cool beers. Try to avoid cider if you can – it looks a bit studenty/country bumpkinish and gives you bad gas. Just before eating, indulge in a few delicious caipirinhas (Brazil's greatest export) or mojitos to whet the appetite. Avoid rich or heavy drinks that could make you feel bilious.

With dinner

Traditionally, you should go for white wine with creamy pasta dishes, poultry, seafood, salads and sushi, but often a chilled rosé or champagne will be even better. If champagne is your favourite tipple, why should you be restricted to special occasions? If you can afford it, drink it.

Choose red wine with tomatoey pasta dishes, meat, pizza and anything with a cheese, chocolate or fruity sauce.

If you find red wine too heavy or white wine too lack-lustre, don't feel forced into following convention. I rebel against white wine in all but the hottest of circumstances, happily ignoring the shocked glances from wine connoisseurs and old ladies, or in Spain I opt for sangria instead. It's a bit *nouveau riche* – but worth it – to chuck a few ice cubes into a warmish glass of white or rosé. Let them tut.

When choosing wine, ask everyone their opinion. Don't storm in just because you've recently been to the Napa Valley. And even if you are the resident expert, don't assume superiority every time you eat out. If there is a genuine wine connoisseur amongst you, ask them to taste the wine (never do this at someone's home!) – it will be to everyone's advantage. If not, go for maturity – ask the oldest person if they'd like to do the sampling. If you find that ageist, let whoever is nearest the wine waiter do the honours. The routine: sniff, swirl and swallow. Don't do any gurgling or spitting.

Post-dinner

With cheese and chocolate, there's nothing nicer than a good port – although your head may hurt the next morning. With ice cream, pie or biscotti, go for a sugary dessert wine like Sauternes. It's expensive, but rewardingly decadent. With coffee, indulge in a warming flame-thrower such as Drambuie, Baileys or Kahlua to get you ready for bed.

Tequila shots and Red Bulls and vodka are perfect if you're planning to go on to a nightclub or party.

In bed

Don't booze. Alcohol is for socialising or de-stressing, neither of which should be a main concern when you're trying to get to sleep. Unwind with a cocoa and a hot bath, and keep a glass of water by your side in case of 'drinker's dawn' – when you wake up early dreaming about liquids after a bit too much of the devil's juice.

How to sober up quickly

Avoid mixing spirits, and if you've got a busy day the next day, stop drinking at midnight. If you've become an incoherent witch and need to sort it out sharpish, take a breather in the loos. Sit on the toilet and refocus. Wash your face (and clean your teeth or chew gum if possible). Check your make-up isn't sliding down your face. Drink as much water as possible to flush it all out and head for the canapés or local takeaway and munch on some carbohydrate. Step outside and get ten minutes' fresh air. If you're still a dribbling wreck, get to bed, you embarrassing bint.

Finally, a good phrase to try and recall is: 'Beer on wine, feel fine. Wine on beer, feel queer.'

Handling a hangover

If you're planning a huge wham-bam of a drinking sesh during the week, don't tell your boss or untrustworthy colleagues. If you need a 'duvet day' the next morning they'll all know why and won't think kindly of you. And anyway, sometimes it's better to get some fresh air and take your mind off it rather than give in and lounge about all day in dirty pyjamas with greasy hair. It's far better to shower, exfoliate, moisturise and put on clean clothes. Don't go for a jog, though – that's just silly!

In our office we can spot a hangover a mile off: the dark-eyed, sloth-like victim stumbles in 15 minutes late with an extra-large coffee, a pint of orange juice and an egg 'n' bacon baguette. This reduces fever, pain and regret until the afternoon, when a second slump hits with force and leaves the sufferer in need of an extra-large tea, an extra-large chocolate muffin and a 15-minute read of *Glamour*. Oh yes, food is all too often the answer. And, as my boss says, anything consumed while you've got a hangover doesn't contain calories(?!), so make it through the day as painlessly as possible.

Secrets of Success

- If there is a cloakroom at the restaurant, put your belongings away – it gives everyone more room to manoeuvre. Tip a small amount per item when you pick them up.

- Flirting at the table is acceptable. Snogging, groping, talking dirty or removing items of clothing is not. Others don't want to be party to your filth. Save it for home time.

◆ Don't cough up food into your napkin – unless you think your life depends on it. If it's just a bit greasy, fatty or lumpy, sorry girls, it's polite to swallow. Just have a glass of water nearby.

◆ Be sensitive to others' food preferences. It's not the best idea in the world to have venison followed by veal when you meet your boss's animal activist wife for the first time.

◆ Not all dining companions like to have their photograph taken while they're eating, so check before you snap. Also, some eateries may be too posh and wish to protect their other diners from your probing flash. You must respect your surroundings.

◆ Before you start dropping plates in your local Greek restaurant, check this is a plate-dropping, touristy taverna and not an elegant diner with good plates.

◆ If someone you are dining with gets an allergic reaction to something, don't panic. Check with them what they think it was and ask the chef. Give them water and offer to take them outside for fresh air, home or to the hospital. Antihistamine tablets are often vital, so try and find some as soon as possible.

◆ If one of your party is being rude to staff, quietly tell them to give it a rest, they're spoiling the atmosphere – or, if you're feeling particularly charming, engross them in a conversation about themselves. Rude people normally love this subject.

◆ The table should only be cleared after the last diner has put down their cutlery. But if you still have a pile of festering plates in front of you ten minutes later, it's permissible to ask the staff to clear away the mess. Never stack them yourselves – it's rarely helpful and can be messy. To show you have finished, put your knife and fork neatly together (at the 5 o'clock position if you're pedantic).

◆ If the designated driver stuck to water, don't make them pay for all your booze. And on every other occasion, if someone drives you all home, you should offer to pay for their meal. They're saving you taxi money, remember.

◆ Always remember to budget tipping into the expense of a night out – you must reward good service fairly. If, like the Queen, you don't carry cash, add it on to your direct debit or credit card receipt.

◆ If you have had a terrible meal, you may not feel obliged to leave anything. But food is the responsibility of the kitchen. If the waiting staff have been polite and apologetic, don't punish them. Leave them a small token of your appreciation.

◆ Don't steal ashtrays or cutlery when eating out, but help yourself to matchboxes – they make great mementoes.

Chapter Seven

Being the hostess with the mostest

THERE ARE FEW GREATER pleasures in life than welcoming loved ones through your door and announcing 'Mi casa es su casa'. It's fun to show off your generosity, cooking skills and garden furniture. But it takes more than a few bottles of wine to make people feel at home in your home.

How to be effortlessly accommodating

The golden rules of hospitality are easy to remember and should be carried out as soon as someone (you want to visit) steps over your threshold.

1. Take your guests' coats/umbrellas/bags so they can sit comfortably. Especially if it's been raining or snowing.

2. Offer a hot or cold drink (even if you only have water or black coffee) within 15 minutes of their arrival. I've been at friends' homes for up to two hours before having to ask for a thirst quencher... That's terribly poor form.

3. Keep your home at a comfortable temperature – don't scrimp on the heating or turn it on full blast so visitors swelter like a fat man in a sauna.

4. Don't disappear when guests arrive. Even if you are in the middle of watching your favourite soap or desperate to go to the loo, at least sit them down and ask them how they are.

5. Keep photos and home videos to a minimum. When people say they don't mind looking through 12 packs of snaps from your recent holiday, they're lying. When showing photos, edit them first and don't tell a story with each one. No one finds them as interesting as you do.

6. If guests stay for longer than an hour, offer them something to eat. But if you haven't invited them for a meal, don't go to town. In case of such emergencies, keep a stock of biscuits (if you can resist them. I can't – they'd be gone the first day).

7. If visitors smoke, provide them with an ashtray. Or, if it's a non-smoking house, show them out to the back garden and offer a chair and/or umbrella if it's rainy.

8. Keep plenty of clean towels, toilet paper and a waste-paper basket in your bathroom. Try to make sure the lock works. Transparent doors are never a good idea... they make it very hard to pee.

9. Try not to be in your pyjamas (or naked) after 11 a.m. in case unexpected visitors pop by. And maintain minimum cleanliness around your home – no dirty knickers in the kitchen, etc.

10. Don't make your visitors compete with the television. If there is a programme on you'd like to see, set the video recorder and turn the box off.

The above rules should be applied without question – anything less would be rude and disconcerting. You might as well erect a 'Keep away: visitors beware' sign at your gate. Do want to live a lonely, friendless existence? Thought not... and with a little care and attention, your friends should well and truly consider themselves at home.

Nice little tricks to add to your hostess repertoire:

♦ Keep a supply of quality air-fresheners and scented candles. You can even buy wonderful room sprays which smell of freshly-baked bread, coffee or cinnamon and orange to make your home delicious.

♦ Buy yourself fresh flowers every week if you can afford them – a treat for you and your guests.

♦ Fill your bathroom with soaps, perfumes and hand creams (and a supply of the latest magazines).

♦ Always have a bottle of white wine chilling in the fridge and a decent red in the wine rack. Remember to have ice, lemon and mixers to hand.

♦ Some people don't drink caffeine, so have a selection of herbal teas and de-caff coffees and sodas in the kitchen.

♦ Even if visitors insist they're not peckish, leave a bowl of chocolates/nuts/crisps on the table for everyone to share if you know they are coming.

◆ Show how happy you are to see them – give them a hug and thank them for visiting.

The welcome pack

When friends or family have been invited to stay overnight (or longer), the more at home you make them feel, the more you can relax and get on with your own life.

◆ Show them around the kitchen, bathroom and guest bedroom. (If you don't have a spare bedroom, invest in a sofa bed and easy-to-store linen.)

◆ Give them spare keys and show how the doors and windows lock if they're staying for a while.

◆ Encourage them to make their own drinks, snacks, etc.

◆ Clean sheets are a must, as are comfy pillows – and extra blankets should be kept in a cupboard for cold nights.

◆ Leave clean towels at the end of their bed.

◆ Make sure the guest bedroom has a lamp for late-night reading.

◆ A spare alarm clock is helpful, and make sure the curtains or blinds are adequate in case they have time for a lie-in.

◆ Keep a selection of books and magazines out for perusal.

◆ Perhaps install a second television in case of conflicting schedules.

◆ Leave the iron, hairdryer and telephone in mutually helpful areas.

◆ Tell your guests you have spare razors, tweezers, nail files, etc., if they've forgotten anything. Never run low on shampoo, conditioner and delicious bubble bath. Stock up on headache pills, indigestion tablets, sanitary products and plasters. Each time you stay at a good hotel, take the mini toiletries, toothbrushes, shower caps and sewing kits home.

◆ Keep wastepaper baskets in the spare bedroom and the bathroom.

◆ Outline your routine and diary for as long as your guests are staying, so they know when they can have some privacy or when they can catch up with you.

◆ Make it clear that even though you wish to retire at 11 p.m., they can stay up as long as they wish and show them how to turn off all the lights, etc.

◆ At bedtime, offer a jug of water/hot water bottle/herbal sleeping pills.

A guest too far...

However, your hospitality should not extend to long-distance phone calls, a ransacking of your drinks cabinet, illegal substances entering your home, strangers being allowed to wander around your hallways in the middle of the night or sexual favours. Generally, guests should feel at home *but* not behave as if they're in their own home. It's all about respect.

Unwanted guests

It's great to catch up with the gang – but on your own terms...

If friends show up at your door when you're really not in the mood to entertain, get rid of them quick. It's better to tell a few white lies than tarnish your hostess reputation forever.

If it's really not convenient, tell them so – but insist you get out your diaries to fix a date straightway. If you just can't be bothered, pretend a) you've got a nasty illness and it's catching (sneeze, cough, make frequent trips to the lavatory), b) you're on your way out (when you see them walking up the path or through the keyhole, pull on your coat, grab your keys and make like a person in a rush), or c) invite them in but don't observe the golden rules listed above. They'll feel unwelcome and leave (unless they have a skin as thick as a rhino's hide, in which case revert to plans a) or b).

NB Remember, if you really don't want company, or feel the state of the bathroom would have your mother cursing you for days, you don't have to answer the door. Spy-holes are wonderful things.

Guests who outstay their welcome

It's fun to be sociable, but even the most altruistic of domestic goddesses will want some downtime every now and again. Stray-dog friends are a nightmare. How long should they be allowed to stay for?

If you invite people for dinner, it is perfectly acceptable

to offer a final round of coffees at 11 p.m. on a work-night and midnight at the weekend. Of course, if the conversation is still sparkling and you feel bright-eyed and bushy-tailed, encourage your friends to stay as long as they wish. If you've been yawning since midnight but your guests are still yapping at 2 a.m., get into your pyjamas or start doing the washing up by all means.

MARTHA, 29

❝ I have a terrible habit of just taking myself off to bed ... but our guests feel so contented they carry on drinking and debating with my husband anyway. If you're happy to get the party started then leave it going, escape when you feel you'd put a downer on the evening. ❞

If you have invited people to stay overnight, make sure you have a hearty breakfast ready for them – and a selection of newspapers would be great too. Don't wake them, unless you need to be somewhere urgently or it's after midday. When they rise, show them how the shower works, etc., then prepare coffee, toast and any other delights you have in the cupboard. Polite guests will leave shortly afterwards.

If your guests aren't showing any sign of budging, drop hints about your busy day ahead. If they're still sitting gormlessly on the sofa by the afternoon, just ask them to go. You don't have to be rude – in fact you can bemoan the fact you can't sit and chat all day but the laundry won't do itself. We once had a friend who came to a New Year's Eve party and didn't leave until 2nd January... My husband and I felt exhausted and grumpy when he finally left and wished we'd had the sense to show him the door 24 hours earlier.

If people actually ask to stay for a while, set an agreed time and make them stick to it. And remember, you can always refuse – your home is *your* sanctuary. We once had guests for two months who were still there eight months later and we were all quite stressed by the end. So think up 'house rules' as soon as people arrive, get a spare set of keys cut so you don't have to work around each other and accept reasonable offers of financial or domestic help. This will leave you two fewer things to resent when you start to regret having such an open house. Without realising it, having other people – even family – in your home puts you under a lot of pressure, so don't feel bad about saying it's not convenient. And remember, your family aren't anyone else's family. Your partner won't be as keen to share his home with your wayward sister as you will.

Dinner parties

Staying in is the new going out. People love to be at home where they can relax rather than venturing out into expensive, flash bistros filled with idiots and psychopaths, or fighting their way through the traffic and bad weather to attend the ballet. So why not hold a dinner party? It's a great way to socialise and you can direct the evening the way you would like it to go – well, until the guests arrive late, the food gets burnt and someone pours a glass of red wine on your new beige carpet. And some rude friends haven't even bought a bottle. Honestly! Why are you bothering?

Have faith in the reasons below and you'll get through it:

1. You can look a mess and no one cares – and if you actually look fabulous everyone congratulates you.

2. You don't have to put up with rude waiters and bad service.

3. You can choose the menu and the music.

4. You don't have to wait for a taxi or a parking space.

5. You can fine-tune your cooking skills.

Inviting people

When inviting someone to a social gathering, make sure you give them plenty of warning (unless it's an informal supper party), ask them for any food no-nos (write down what they can't eat if planning a long time in advance), state the dress code, the time to arrive and the time to dine (i.e. 'arrive 7.30 p.m. for 8 p.m. dinner') and maybe who you've invited – especially if you have an ex-president, supermodel or *Pop Idol* finalist coming who you want to show off about.

For dinner parties, it's normal to invite people face to face or over the phone and allow them a few days to check their diaries before they confirm.

If you wish to post invites, put 'RSVP' at the bottom and chase attendees if they still haven't replied within a few weeks of the gathering – just in case it's slipped their mind and they show up unannounced and have to eat beans on toast.

SUE, 41

❝ Recently at a dinner party, my friend was feeling a bit miffed because she was going to Spain for the weekend and would miss another's party. She said, very seriously, "When

inviting people to parties, it is etiquette to give six weeks"
notice – anything less implies you're not bothered whether
your invitee can come or not.' So at the ripe old age of 40
something I learnt something new and now give my guests
plenty of warning. 🍃

Guest list – getting the mix right

When hosting an intimate soirée, it is important to fine-tune
the guest list to allow the greatest pleasure for all. If two
friends have had a nasty fight, don't get them along on the
same night – you'll be too busy to play peacemaker. Also,
think where the most fun for you lies: perhaps balance
some duller colleagues you must entertain with some fun
old friends you can trust to be sociable and exciting – they'll
take the pressure off you. Other tips:

◆ If you fancy a relaxed night, stick with those you know
best.

◆ Avoid inviting three couples who know each other well
and then a random twosome – the new pair will feel left
out or be bored to tears by your group's anecdotes. Do
have faith in your mates, though.

◆ Never panic unduly about seating a fascist (you know
one?) next to a socialist – it could make for an interesting
evening.

◆ Warn your other guests if there are any absolutely no-go
areas, i.e. someone has recently been widowed, divorced
or lost a child.

HELEN, 35

❝ Too many invitations to return? When making a dinner-party list, divide it into your A-list (owe-an-invite) and your B-list (just-for-pleasure). Send out your A-list a few weeks before your B-list. That way you know you've invited all the priority guests and you can then fill up from your B-list. The only problem is having two friends who are quite close. One will say to the other, "Are you going to...?" and the other will say, 'I don't know anything about it.' This could lead to a bit of a falling out because she wasn't on the A-list. All very complicated. Best thing to do is never throw a party. ❞

The day of the dinner party

You may think a supper soirée is all about food, but there are other things to consider when you are planning a perfect evening:

◆ Check you have clean napkins, tablecloth and polished cutlery. Get them out the day before and make sure. This will give you enough time to rectify any problems.

◆ Dust the rooms you will be entertaining in and spray some pleasant fragrances around.

◆ Store away things you don't want to be seen in your bedroom – the one room no guest should wander into.

◆ Plan where you will put visitors' coats. If you don't have a coat rack or cupboard, clear the bed in a spare room and put them on there.

◆ Draw up a seating plan if you think it best.

♦ Peruse your drinks cabinet – you should never rely on guests to bring their own wine or assume people won't drink much. Decent people will bring a couple of decent bottles, but keep a good few as back-up. Also check after-dinner liqueurs haven't gone past their consume-by date. Remember lemon, lime, ice, straws and stirrers too.

♦ Table decorations can add the final touch to a perfect evening. Think about candles, flowers, glitter and, for a super-special occasion, little gifts.

♦ Music needs to be chosen carefully. Once you've made your selection, place the CDs next to the stereo so you don't forget to put it on.

♦ Entertainment? Invest in a selection of board games and perhaps (here comes the Essex in me) a karaoke machine for those spontaneously lively nights.

♦ Your outfit should be planned before you start cooking, so you can prepare the food and then quickly shower, dress and get made up an hour before everyone descends on you ... and look as cool and calm as Gwyneth Paltrow (we can try!)

♦ If you're going to allow smoking, plan where and how. Stock up on scented candles and ashtrays or arrange some chairs outside for the smokers.

♦ There should always be a clean bed on offer in case a visitor is taken ill.

♦ Remember, if someone accepts an invite to your home, they should be rewarded with a great time. OK, so you've done the cooking and the cleaning, but they've made the leap of faith and the journey.

Tut, tut – bad hostess!

A modern hostess with the mostest should always:

◆ Introduce her guests, even if she assumes they have met before.

◆ Accept the offer of help in the kitchen if she suspects a friend fancies a chat (or wants to escape her boyfriend's creepy brother).

◆ Keep glasses replenished.

◆ Give the co-host (if there is one) a reasonable list of concerns.

◆ Keep her make-up bag in the downstairs loo to touch up her face when it's all got steamy.

◆ Offer the nice wine and chocolates a guest has brought (unless they are of such poor quality it is obvious the bearer was looking for a cheap night out).

◆ Not make a big deal about clearing up (even if you will wash 'n' dry before going to bed, tell kind guests not to worry and you'll leave it until morning).

◆ Not feel cross about doing the washing-up – even when guests offer to help, they may feel aggrieved if they are actually handed a tea-towel.

Pets

Not everyone thinks animals are magic. Be sure to keep pets and pet areas away from your guests, and only unleash animals if you are 100 per cent certain they will be well received. It's funny, but people really don't like having their crotch sniffed or face licked whilst enjoying a social glass of champagne. Also, work out if your house has a lingering pet odour – often you'll be so used to it you can't detect it, but it may well put off diners.

> **NB If you hate or are allergic to animals**, it is far more polite to check ahead about their presence and take precautions accordingly (i.e. suggest a neutral location, don't go or take an allergy tablet) than to turn up only to have an awful time.

Children

Similarly, some people aren't mad on children. Indeed, until you become a parent yourself, it's hard to understand the appeal of these squeaky, short things who cry and puke a lot.

Never show up to a dinner party with your kids in tow unless you have checked in advance that it's OK. And don't be offended if the answer is 'no' – people want to spend time talking to you, not watching you change nappies. Enjoy having a night without the little ones for once.

If you are giving a party and you have children, bribe the over-fives to stay upstairs with a takeaway of choice and a DVD to watch in their room and pray the babies don't wake up.

Can't cook, won't cook ... must cook

Some people excel in the kitchen and look forward to developing signature dishes for their lucky guests. But most of us need a free afternoon and a celebrity chef's cook book to prepare even the most basic of recipes. So how can you avoid giving your friends and family food poisoning?

1. Don't be overambitious. A simple spaghetti bolognese done well is always better than a duck *à l'orange* done badly.

2. Practise on someone you don't need to impress – your boyfriend/husband/flatmate won't care as long as he's fed.

3. Choose one course that can be easily prepared and refrigerated/frozen the night before – homemade soup or profiteroles and chocolate sauce, for example.

4. Cheat. If the idea of doing three courses really terrifies you, visit your local supermarket. Some ready-prepared dishes are tasty, easy and often cheaper to buy than make from scratch. Glam them up with extras: fresh herbs, sauces or grated cheese.

5. Make one course a non-cook course: cheese and biscuits, tomato and mozzarella salad, fresh berries and cream, etc.

6. Write a full list of ingredients before you hit the shops – you don't want to forget anything in a fluster – and buy a little more than you need in case of emergency.

7. Everyone needs a back-up plan: have a few takeaway menus indoors.

8. If you're not used to hosting big soirées, don't invite more than six people on the first few occasions.

9. Leave nibbles out in case dinner takes a bit longer than planned – fainting guests are soooooo irritating. But do think about timing. Allow 30 minutes to eat a starter and serve the main course an hour after putting the first course on the table. You can play dessert by ear.

10. Don't get tipsy until the main course is safely on the table. Then sink a glass of wine and congratulate yourself for daring to host such an evening – even if the carrots are soggy and the Pavlova hasn't defrosted properly.

If your guests are flagging...

- Keep the booze flowing – the sozzled have fun wherever they are.

- Turn up the music and get the extroverts dancing – the quiet ones can laugh at them.

- Tell people how happy you are to see them – they'll feel flattered.

- Get your camera out and ask guests to pose – ditto.

- Dig out your cocktail shaker and recipe book – and start inventing.

- Open some windows – get that fresh air circulating.

- Admit defeat – offer to book people taxis and get their coats.

If your guests are annoying...

- Put the drunks to bed or order a taxi and shove them in it – they won't remember your stern words and will probably ring to apologise in the morning.

- Smile at the guests who show up with nothing and thank the Lord you're not as ungrateful or mean as that – but don't say anything to their face.

- When two guests start to argue, defuse the situation by offering another round of drinks or suggesting you move into another room, then leap into the seat between them and change the subject.

- Tardiness is annoying when you're preparing food – don't wait for latecomers until the dinner is ruined. Polite people will ring and let you know what time they should arrive and will understand if you have to go ahead without them.

♦ Almost worse are guests who arrive too early – sit them down with the remote control and some nibbles while you continue your preparations, or take their offer of help if they won't get in the way.

Drinks parties

Sometimes cooking is way too formal or scary to contemplate. Modern girls with an aversion to the kitchen should think about hosting a cocktail or fancy dress party instead.

Drink to success

Gathering friends together for a few bevvies is cheaper and easier to prepare than a sit-down meal, but will still give you the opportunity to show off what you do best: dazzling and sparkling everyone into a good time. Just don't force-feed cheese straws, slow dance in the middle of the room on your own or flirt with your friend's husband.

Cocktail (mover and) shaker

♦ By tradition, cocktail parties are short and sweet and held early on so guests can get elsewhere for dinner, so between 7 and 9 p.m. is a good time. Don't drag it out or people will get drunk and hungry and the atmosphere will flatten.

♦ Don't go mad with the drinks cabinet – the key word here is 'elegant', so choose a colour scheme perhaps and make a signature cocktail. Buy enough ingredients for each guest to have four cocktails each.

- Of course some won't be drinking, so chill water and fruit juice and, if you can, get inventing a non-alcoholic cocktail. Mixing grenadine, juice, soda and crushed ice in equal parts is a good start. Fizzy drinks aren't very sophisticated.

- Some freaks – mainly men – won't like cocktails. So supply enough red and white wine for an average of two glasses per person (you can keep unopened bottles for a later date) or, if you're feeling flash, champagne would make the bash go with a swing.

- Theme drinks to the time of year: egg nog or mulled wine at Christmas, sangria or piña coladas in summer, chocolate martinis at Easter.

- Remember, long cocktails last longer – and are less potent – than short cocktails, so stick with those. And avoid things that need more than four ingredients and take ages to prepare.

- Send out invites if you don't want waifs and strays. If you just say 'I'm having a drinks party', guests will assume it's OK to bring along a hanger-on.

- Don't allow friends to bring their children unless you specifically want that sort of evening – even babies who are put upstairs could spoil the night if they start screaming.

- Music should be low-key and interesting – samba, salsa, DJ mixes...

- Although you're holding a 'drinks' party, if people are coming straight from work they'll be famished, so serve simple canapés. If you're not hiring staff, organise food that can be left on a table and doesn't need to be carried round on trays – delicious breads, olives, cold meats, cheeses, chocolate-dipped strawberries, etc. You don't really need the hassle of sorting out cutlery, so put things on sticks and distribute paper napkins. Supermarkets produce fantastic finger food at reasonable prices if you can't be bothered to chop a thing. Don't serve anything too oniony, fishy or garlicky.

♦ Pick the venue carefully. If your home is too small to swing a cat, let alone a dancing partner, hire the private room of a restaurant, beg a family member to let you borrow their castle or be original and hold the event in a museum, shop, park, etc.

♦ With a drinks party, you're saving cash on food but you're inviting more guests, so still be financially prepared to be a perfect host. If money is tight, it's better to invite fewer guests than invite the world and his dog.

House parties

You've drunkenly announced at the pub one night, 'I'm having a party at my house – it will be fabulous. The more the merrier.' Now your friends are ringing to ask if they can bring anything and they're looking forward to it. Oh shit! You've never held a big thang before… What can you do?

♦ If there are lots of people coming who have never met, set a theme. Either go to town on the décor (there'll be lots to talk about) or insist on fancy dress (there'll be lots to laugh at). Popular themes are: eighties, toga, bad taste, tarts and vicars (yes, still!), superheroes, come as your favourite thing, come as a celebrity…

- Give your party a purpose: Halloween, your birthday, Christmas... That way everyone will know loosely what to expect.

- Invest in, borrow or hire some interesting lighting – people are more inclined to dance with flashing strobes or a mirror ball on the dance floor.

- Prepare your music well before. If you've arranged a DJ or live music, brief them on must-plays and must-nots. If you're making tapes/playlists, get as wide a mix as possible, but don't do a slow section (it will bring back all kinds of unwanted-at-school-discos nightmares for your guests). Keep it upbeat, don't leave long gaps between songs and avoid those tunes you really can't stand. It's your party, after all.

- Make sure there's lots of loo roll in the toilets.

- And keep local taxi numbers to hand for when guests wish to leave.

- There'll always be a few who have a few too many... Try and get rid of them before they start shouting or fighting. Put them to bed, shove them in a taxi or take them outside for a serious word and a glass of water. Always have a few sensible, burly friends on hand who you can rely on to help.

- Food isn't a concern at such parties – a few bowls of nachos, nuts and nibbles should do it. Lollipops and sweets are a fun alternative.

- Think about keeping drinks near the dance area to encourage boogieing – people always congregate around the booze, which is why kitchens are often the hippest hangouts.

◆ Lacking space to chill drinks at home? Fill the bath with ice and leave them there.

The best party in the world ever

Be original and your 'do' will be the stuff of legend. Think about serving breakfast (something as simple as bacon rolls) to flagging guests at midnight, or set up fireworks. Make party bags filled with balloons, streamers, hats and blowers. Hire a special guest performer – a comedian or an impersonator. Leave DJ request slips on the tables so guests feel they can control the music. Cover the ceiling in fairy lights and dust tables with glitter. Allow easy access to drinks, toilets and fresh air. Flowers will be a waste of time and money in a smoky, dark atmosphere so spend the cash on ice sculptures or water features instead. Hire coloured glasses and leave cocktail shakers around so guests can experiment.

LISA, 26

❝ I went to an eighties fancy dress party last year. Everyone had made an effort – lots of deely-boppers, 'Frankie Says Relax' T-shirts and shoulder-pads. The hosts had covered their house in posters – even building a Madonna shrine in the toilet – and served Liebfraumilch and cheese 'n' pineapple sticks. They gave everyone nametags for easy introductions and organised pass-the-parcel (with funny prizes) and dancing competitions. None of this cost a lot of money, but they'd put a lot of thought into it and it showed. I danced till dawn. ❞

When the party's over...

Allow yourself a few days to recover – don't accept invitations to lunch or dinner the next day. You deserve a lie-in, a long soak in the bath and a box of chocolates while watching *Grease* for the hundredth time. Do not – on the spur of the 'party' moment – invite people back to your house the next day for snacks and a catch-up. Even if the party was a great success, you won't want to see your guests for at least a week.

The only chores are getting the venue back in shape (think about hiring help if you're on your own) and calling people to say thanks for bringing food, lights, music, etc. When all that is done, switch on the answering machine. Your polite friends will be calling to offer their congratulations, but take time to recover before talking to them. If someone rings with a snide remark, however, don't take it lying down. If they're rude about your hosting skills, reply, 'I can't wait to be invited to your house then, it will surely be fantastic.' If they are rude about a fellow guest, say, 'It's a shame you feel like that, they said the loveliest thing about you...' And remember, satisfaction comes from not being rude to the rude person.

Secrets of Success

♦ The night before the bash, think about who you want to introduce to each other, who would get on, who wouldn't, etc.

♦ Remember to eat something before your party starts – booze, stress and business can be dangerous.

- If you're nervous about your party getting started, call on your closest girlfriends to arrive early with their dancing shoes on.

- Make a good impression from the moment your guests arrive. Sprinkle petals and tea lights around the bathroom and garden (in good weather), and dim lighting to eat by candlelight. Scatter cushions and drapes can be relaxing too.

- Don't allow guests to criticise your taste in home décor. They shouldn't be so rude – and this includes your parents and in-laws.

- Similarly, don't adjust your personal style to suit others. The only exception is if your guest is a new boyfriend. Remove the knick-knacks of past boyfriends until you know each other better.

- Learn what is fulfilling your hostess duties and what is over the top. If a guest says they're not hungry or thirsty, believe them.

- If you're serving canapés, allow 10–15 per head for a two-hour drinks party.

- Don't be a tight-arse. Being the perfect hostess is an expensive business, but worth it for the praise you'll receive. Don't ruin a nice dinner by serving bad wine or limp salad.

- Traditionally when planning who sits where, engaged couples sit next to each other, while married couples should always be seated apart. The hosts should sit at the top of the table. If possible, place each guest next to at least one person they've met a few times before.

- Don't decorate the dinner table with overpowering flowers (guests won't be able to smell the food) and cut out the stamens if you have lilies – they're lethal.

◆ At intimate dinners, sit loudmouths next to wallflowers for balance.

◆ Some social experts suggest moving round the table between courses. Judge the mood on the night. Sometimes it just pisses people off when they're in the middle of an interesting conversation.

◆ It's nice to offer guests a dessertspoon *and* fork. Place them above the plates, perpendicular to the other cutlery.

◆ Accidents will happen – have a carpet cleaner handy to remove stains as quickly as possible. A dustpan and brush isn't a bad idea either. And don't let it spoil your mood – casualties are the expected downside of hostessing.

◆ If someone drops out at the last minute, fill the gap with a faithful friend – but be honest about why you asked them. They won't mind as long as they're prepared.

◆ Keep track of people you owe invites to and 'payback' within a year.

◆ As the hostess, you should expect to have a good time but don't expect to sit around and catch up with your friends. You'll be lucky to take the weight off your feet for a few minutes.

◆ Do make the effort to look good – if the hostess doesn't look fabulous, why should her guests? Get that apron off, for starters!

Chapter Eight

Being the perfect guest

THIS IS EASY – it just boils down to R E S P E C T. Find out what it means to you and others when you become a visitor to their home. Make yourself at home, sure – no one wants an uncomfortable stiff in their sitting-room – but treat other people's homes as their castles and live by their rules.

How to get invited back

The best guests are those who understand their stay is putting people out – none of us like to have our routines broken and having a newcomer in the mix causes headaches, even if you all know each other very well. So take nothing for granted. Be pleasant at all times, so your host or hostess finds you a fun companion rather than an irritating chore.

Here's an example of what not to do: a close friend of mine held a pool party a few years ago and some bad guests fed her dog cannabis in a sausage. The dog didn't seem to mind too much – although he did keep walking into the patio furniture – but the hostess spent the rest of the afternoon in a panic. This was such a bad situation to put her in ... but she was such a good hostess so tried to laugh it off and not make the offenders feel guilty.

SASHA, 29

❝ My worst, worst, worst type of guest is the one who comes to your home bringing a bottle of wine as a gift. They stay a few hours, you feed them, crack open the booze, then the chocolates, then more booze ... and when they get up to leave they say, "Oh, you didn't drink my wine. I'll take it back then," and shuffle out through the door clutching it under their arm. This behaviour doesn't compute with me at all. I have one friend who has done this a few times – I've even caught her hiding her bottle in a cupboard and then retrieving it at the end of the night to take home again. She's probably had the same bottle doing the circuit for five years now, and it really makes me resentful. ❞

The key things to remember are:

◆ Don't make surprise visits – people could be ill, asleep or copulating.

◆ Don't arrive over half an hour early or half an hour late without a warning phone call.

◆ Do take a gift, even if you're not expecting dinner. People should feed and water you even if you stay an hour, so offer something in return. Something as simple or cheap as a nice photo or packet of biscuits will do.

◆ Don't ask colleagues or people you have known less than a year to put you up for a few nights – it's a huge imposition.

◆ Don't insult someone's home. Even something as subtle as 'I wouldn't have chosen those colours' is extremely rude.

◆ Don't help yourself to food or drink before you are offered it.

◆ Don't nose through private belongings or go into someone's bedroom.

> **NB There is an argument** – I suppose – that friends and family should not have to bring anything to your house. As a good hostess, you will have ample food and water for all. But that's missing the point. You'll get a reputation as a tight-arse if you don't show gratitude... and the invites will start drying up.

Return to sender

When replying to an invite, give a 'yes' or 'no' answer asap – no 'maybes'! Such answers are rude to the hosts and can slow down their impeccable planning. Dinner parties, for example, take a long time to organise.

Never forget to RSVP and then just show up on the night. No reply equals no cocktails or dinner for you, you impolite madam.

Never show up to a dinner with an extra and if you want to bring someone along to a bigger soirée, check first.

If you can't make it at the last minute, inform your host immediately.

Here's how to help your host and hostess to have a good time:

1. Arrive on time, with a generous amount of wine and ask if they need any help.

2. Be sociable. If the host or hostess is elsewhere, introduce the other guests and chat.

3. Don't try and upstage the hosts – this is their evening.

4. Compliment the food, décor, anything you genuinely admire.

5. Don't tell racist, sexist or homophobic jokes, but do discuss politics and religion.

6. Don't demand to be centre of attention – let the others get a word in if it comes up.

7. Befriend the fellow guest who looks a bit lonesome – it will stop the host worrying.

8. Get merry and perky (not drunk and loud).

9. If it's supposed to be a fun, social evening, don't network all night.

10. Be aware of people's needs – if your hosts look at the clock twice in five minutes, it's time to go.

The morning-after drill

You must always follow up a pleasant evening with an e-mail, call, letter or bunch of flowers, depending on how long you've stayed for. This will help your hosts realise it was all worth it... when they're left coping with a mountain of dirty plates and a lounge that smells like a pub.

Returning the favour

As you leave, you should insist on having your host or hostess round for dinner (or taking them out for dinner if your kitchen is a disaster). There's no need to set dates immediately, but make a note to self to follow-up the offer in a few weeks' time.

When you become a semi-permanent guest (moving in for a week or more), you must accept you are permanently indebted to the person you're staying with. They can now ring and ask to stay with you and you should – except in difficult circumstances – welcome them with open arms (although they shouldn't take advantage).

DAISY, 27

❛ To save a few quid, I stayed at a friend's house overnight when I went to a wedding in her neck of the woods. Three months later, she was on the blower saying she was coming to look for work in London and could I put her up for a few weeks? To pay my dues, I said she could stay for three nights while she got settled and then she must move on. I explained I had a tiny flat and lots of studying to do for work and she seemed OK about it. I'm glad I was upfront rather than resenting her afterwards. ❜

Staying for a few days

If you're staying for a few days, the pressure is on. The best guests leave after five hours, so staying a few nights could rock the boat. Best friends have been known to fall out over wet towels left on the floor. Here's how to save your friendship while keeping a roof over your head:

◆ As soon as you walk through the door, say thank you. Again and again.

◆ Take a special gift – a box of chocolates won't do. Choose a significant book or CD, a photo frame or a bouquet of the host's favourite flowers.

◆ Put your belongings in your room immediately. Leave as few signs you are there as possible.

◆ Stay neat and tidy. Don't leave dirty plates in the kitchen for someone else to clear up.

◆ Be out as much as is socially acceptable. Obviously, you shouldn't treat the house like a hotel, but allow the residents to have time alone.

◆ Don't rely on your host for transport. Check out local trains and buses.

◆ If other people are coming over, offer to make yourself scarce.

◆ Use your senses. If you can pick up on an irritable vibe, take yourself off to bed for an early night.

◆ Ask about their routine so you don't appear rude. It might be best not to stay up all night watching television and then sleep all day.

◆ Don't stay in the bathroom longer than necessary. Shower, yes. Two-hour soak in the bath, no. If the hot water is running out, tell them.

◆ Be thoughtful: pick up fresh fruit, flowers and chocolates for everyone to enjoy.

◆ Offer to help pay bills or housekeeping. And don't be shocked if it's accepted – people could be on a tight budget and staying with them will still be cheaper than a hotel.

◆ Offer to make dinner and to wash up on the nights you're not cooking. Offer to change the bedsheets when you leave.

◆ If you are staying longer than three nights, take your hosts out for dinner.

The parent trap

Being the guest of a family member should be easy. You've known them all your life, you share common ground and you know what drives them mad. But familiarity can breed contempt. Because you *do* know each other so well, social etiquette goes out the window. While staying with my parents, I revert to being a stroppy 13-year-old. I fight with my brothers and play pop music loudly while they shake their heads with disappointment.

Sometimes, though, reverting to type is the best thing with your parents – you'll all know where you stand. Just minimise stress by offering help around the house, buying a thank-you present and asking their opinions – three things you probably never did when you lived there permanently.

Staying with other family members won't be so difficult.

(Why is it only mums and dads that can frustrate and torment you into such a frenzy?) But don't expect your partner to be as thrilled about a clan visit as you are – especially one that lasts more than three hours. Families are strange enough when you belong to one – they get even weirder when you're an outsider looking in.

Embarrassing dilemmas for the modern houseguest

How to cover up life's mishaps and misdemeanours...

Royal flush

Going to the toilet in the night can cause all kinds of problems – to flush or not to flush, that is the question. If you do a number two, flush whatever the hour. People would rather be woken by water than frightened by an evil pong when they go to do their ablutions. Just put the seat down and keep the door shut until the noise of the flush passes. If someone's bedroom is next to the bathroom and you just need a wee, lay toilet paper on the water surface and exit. Flushing is fine after 8 a.m.

Sex crime

Having sex in someone else's house is another tricky thing. We recently had guests shagging so loudly it kept us awake all night and made breakfast pretty awkward. If you're away for one night, control yourself. You won't die going without it for 24 hours. If you're away for longer, the key is to do it quietly – even going on the floor if it's a creaky bed or waiting till the hosts are out for an hour if you're dating a screamer. Don't leave condoms lying about and keep the sheets as clean as possible. Leaving them for your hosts to deal with is taking their hospitality too far.

Bloody bad luck

Getting your period while you're away from home is a nightmare at the best of times – you feel ill, cry a lot and shout at people on the television. If you feel emotional, keep yourself to yourself and have lots of early nights. If you leak on the sheets, be honest and ask to wash them yourself as soon as possible. We've all been there. Every good hostess should have a cupboard stocked with emergency tampons and painkillers, so don't suffer in silence. Good hostesses should also have a bin in their bathroom for easy sanitary product disposal – if not, tie them up in a plastic bag and deposit them in the dustbin when you can.

Toilet humour

Making a mess in the bathroom can be red-cheek inducing. No good guest would dream of leaving skid marks in someone else's toilet. First of all check out the loo brush situation: thank the heavens if there is one and prepare for a nasty moment if there isn't. Arm yourself with a thick wad of toilet paper, flush the loo for a second time and violently scrub while holding your nose with your other hand.

Naked truth

Getting caught naked is mortifying. Grab a tablecloth, coat, napkin, anything to cover your modesty. If there's nothing to hand, adopt a bent leg, crouching position and use both hands to cover your boobs. Yell 'Oh God, please turn round!' and make your exit and then apologise when you're fully clothed. If you catch your host or hostess naked, escape immediately without laughing and don't refer to the incident unless they bring it up.

Accidental tourist

When visiting friends, accidents will happen even if you're very careful and sober. I had an embarrassingly clumsy moment last year. Over dinner, my husband knocked over a glass of red wine on our friend's cream carpet. I quickly leapt up to help clean it (and tell him off), only to send the rest of the bottle flying. The carpet was covered. Without thinking, I grabbed a bottle of vintage Chablis the hostess had been saving for a special occasion and poured it over the red to stop it staining. It didn't... We left our mark in more ways than one that evening. Thankfully, they are lovely people. They could see we were mortified – we scrubbed for ages and offered to pay whatever it took to make it right – and they accepted our sincerest apologies... and haven't stopped laughing about it since. So if you ever do break or stain something while being a guest, be honest about it, work hard to make it better and then offer to reimburse any damage. The same applies for cigarette burns (if you are a smoker, stay outside or near an ashtray at all times).

Love changes everything

If any of your hosts ever makes a pass at you, refuse firmly and avoid being left alone in the house again. Don't tell tales unless you think your disturbing news will do more good than harm and don't tell your partner while you're still staying there. Do not think, 'Phwoar, all right then,' and jump into bed. This is abusing hospitality to the highest degree. In general, it's unwise to stay with anyone you know fancies you. Your sense of gratitude could get you into all sorts of trouble... and that person will only be along the hallway.

JILL, 33

❝ It really pisses me off when guests turn up to stay for a night (or longer) empty-handed. I always serve champagne at dinner if we have company, put fresh flowers in the guest bedroom and go out of my way to make them feel welcome. I am shocked when people turn up without even so much as a sniff of a flower or a bottle – even a bottle of plonk. Let's face it – even if they are good friends, surely reciprocation is the name of the game. I would never dream of going anywhere without taking something with me, but there you go! I've got manners. ❞

Escape route

Being a guest isn't all it's cracked up to be. Sometimes you're climbing the walls in search of a quick exit. If you do feel your social decorum is about to expire, get out before you turn offensive. Follow these cunning plans...

Friends' parties

Sometimes being the guest of close friends isn't about being pampered and looked after. Sure, you're at their party, but you've become part of the furniture, your empty glass and grumbling stomach go unnoticed and you want to scream:

'I'm a friend, get me outta here!'

♦ Say 'hello' to everyone you know and slip out quietly without saying goodbye. They'll know they saw you at some stage in the evening but won't remember when.

♦ Act drunk. Everyone's grateful when a slurring, spitting fool takes themselves off to bed.

♦ Text a friend and ask them to call you with a fake emergency. Move to the middle of the hosts' group and make a big deal about receiving the call.

♦ Blame a nasty boss, a strict fitness instructor or a new baby (if you've got one) for making you tired and unprepared for the next day. Then leave. All girls will understand.

♦ You can always fall back on the classic headache if the music is loud.

> **NB If you really can't make a move** without offence, spend time with your hostess telling her what fun you are having, but keep an eye out for the first people to leave and then follow in their footsteps – the first ones to escape will be remembered as party poopers, not you. Or find a yawning person and ask to share a cab. Look disappointed when they tell you the car has arrived.

Official functions

When you are invited to a special event as a representative of your company or club, things are a little tougher. You can't escape early and you can't avoid certain people. Try to see such gatherings as an extension of your work and look on the bright side – it's not costing you anything, you might make valuable new contacts and you'll win a few Brownie points from your boss.

Before you go, find out:

♦ What the dress code is.

♦ How long you should stay for.

♦ Whether your boss/colleague would like you to be there before the official kick-off to set up, debrief or welcome the other guests.

♦ Whether there is anyone to whom you need to pay special attention.

♦ What conversation topics should or shouldn't be brought up.

Gatecrashing

If, on the other hand, you just love parties, how can you become the Elizabeth Hurley of your local circuit? The easiest way to be on top of the world's guest list is to throw a few stellar bashes yourself. These will show how cool, well connected and fun you are – and people will be desperate to get you along to their own parties!

Alternatively, get a job in a cool bar or pub and you'll soon get acquainted with the hip regulars.

If your name's not on a guest list, you can try to gatecrash: dress up, get your hair done and walk with confidence. Don't travel in packs (get past the doorman on your own or with one equally attractive friend). Or make friends with the kitchen staff and sneak in round the back.

When you do finally get in to a swanky affair, don't embarrass yourself. Stay calm and act like you belong there.

Secrets of Success

◆ When someone opens their door to you, they open their heart. Never take that for granted. Be grateful, polite and helpful – and leave their house as you found it.

◆ Don't make it all about food and sleep. If you're staying for a few days, suggest going out to the cinema, an art gallery or even playing a board game while drinking hot chocolate – anything to make your visit a treat, not a chore.

◆ Never answer someone else's telephone or open their mail unless asked to.

◆ If your hosts are busy decorating, gardening or doing any other major household tasks, offer to lend a hand.

◆ If you have been invited to dinner, give sufficient warning of food preferences or allergies. If you are staying for a few days, bring your own supply of special groceries with you, e.g. soya milk.

◆ If you're staying with someone else, always check before you bring back friends for drinks or to stay overnight – no one wants to bump into a stranger in their hallway.

◆ Guests should maintain personal hygiene at all times. Even if you're prone to hanging around your home in stained pyjamas with your hair all greasy, clean up your act when you're elsewhere. Grime is a crime. I've had guests who have stayed for three nights and not washed once. Opening all the windows, lighting every candle and having a cold couldn't save me from their repellent odour – and I'd consider banning them from my house because of it.

♦ Don't complain about noisy children, over-friendly pets or other people's choice in television when it's their home, not yours.

♦ Take appropriate clothing. Borrowing a jumper or a water-proof is as far as wardrobe sharing should go. You're in their home, keep out of their wardrobe.

♦ Staying for over two weeks but they won't accept your offer of financial help? Buy gift vouchers or a luxury hamper as a present when you leave.

♦ When you are invited to dinner, there is no such thing as fashionably late. Arrive within half an hour of your bene-factor's 'Come at 7.30ish' invite. However, at larger events, arriving late will allow you to make an entrance, get straight on the dance floor, and feel superior when the drunken early-arrivals start turning green around the gills.

♦ Learn from your own guests. Who has annoyed you the least and why? Mimic their positive characteristics when you're in someone else's home.

♦ Enjoy being looked after. Good guests are happy, grateful guests.

Chapter Nine

High days and holidays

WHY DO SO MANY PEOPLE forget how to be socially acceptable when they break from the norm? It seems a trip to a foreign country or a little too much booze at Christmas can turn the most elegant, modern girl into an insolent wreck. Just remember, girls, in good times or bad, home or away, Gene Kelly in *Singin' in the Rain* was right: dignity, always dignity.

The big ones

There are general rules to be obeyed at all important events and special days:

◆ Show up on time.

◆ Sit quietly during the, er, quiet bits.

◆ Don't start fights or vomit into your hat.

◆ Keep an eye on the shy or friendless.

◆ Most likely there will be children and old people there. If so, do not patronise them, ignore them or act as if they are deaf: children have hearing to rival dogs and old people have been there and done it so even if they are deaf, they'll recognise the facial expressions.

◆ Introduce people to one another.

◆ Don't show up with random hangers-on.

◆ Only video or take photographs when permitted.

Weddings

◆ Do not upstage the bride – anything white, lacy, shiny and long is highly inappropriate, as is a veil and a blue suspender belt. It can be elegant to wear black, but check with the bride that she doesn't think it's bad luck.

◆ Even if the bride's dress is not to your taste, be nice about it. It reflects her style and obviously makes her feel confident.

◆ Do not cough or clap during after the 'If anyone here present knows any...' bit – even the most innocent couples get nervous that someone has discovered something to stop them getting hitched.

◆ Do not throw confetti in the grounds if you have been asked not to. Wait till you get outside.

◆ If you've already tied the knot, resist the urge to compare everything with your own day and bore anyone who'll listen with 'I did it better when I...'

◆ Never offer the bride a cigar, cigarette or flaming Drambuie.

◆ Don't pick at the cake before it's been officially cut.

◆ Don't hit the dance floor before the first dance.

◆ Don't go back to the honeymoon suite with the newly-weds, and certainly don't surprise them by going on honeymoon with them.

◆ Try not to cling to the bride or groom – they have a lot of people to talk to.

◆ Some people hate weddings (freaks!) – don't let them suck you down into an 'expensive bloody waste of time' conversation. Have fun ... it's the one time you can dance to silly songs without being embarrassed.

◆ Leave your gifts somewhere considerate and safe – you don't want them to get lost or broken – and mark them clearly with your names. Or stick your card to the gift so they don't get separated.

◆ Support the speechmakers – listen and laugh even if they're not funny.

◆ As you leave, thank the bride's and groom's parents as well as the couple. Even if the couple paid for everything, the parents will have helped host the event.

◆ Cheer up 'the old marrieds' when they return from honeymoon with a letter saying how much fun you had and a couple of photos of the event.

Funerals

◆ Send a card to the family as soon as you hear the news.

◆ Don't ever make the day just about you or your grief – everyone is affected.

◆ Do not arrive at the church/crematorium with music blasting in your car.

◆ Act with decorum at all times.

◆ Offer sincere condolences and memories.

◆ Try not to weep hysterically when you shake hands with the bereaved.

◆ Don't laugh at the floral tributes (even if they say 'BIG BOY' or 'BEST MANAGER' in pink carnations).

◆ Wear colour if it has been requested, black or navy if no mention of clothes has been made. Never wear short skirts or glittery make-up.

◆ If you have a bad cough or cold, sit at the back and leave if necessary during the service.

◆ If the family do not wish to have flowers, make a contribution to a charity instead.

◆ It is polite to attend the wake, even for five minutes.

◆ Take a quiet minute to remember the reason you are there.

Christenings

- If you've been asked to be a godparent, be flattered – and don't turn it down because you fear it will be a huge responsibility. Today, it's a flexible role.

- Take a gift for the baby, even if you've already given the parents something when the child was born. Try to buy something the child can keep: books, jewellery or antiques.

- Even if you are a non-believer, respect the parents' wish to introduce their child to religion.

- Don't automatically laugh or smirk when the child cries at the 'water' bit. Take your lead from the parents and if they find it funny, it's OK.

- Don't laugh or smirk at all if the child is wearing a dress – it's traditional in some religions.

- Even if you're a real child-hater, try and feign enough interest for a brief chat. The baby is why you're all there, after all.

- Don't yawn … yes, the services are long and dull and the seats are uncomfortable, but politeness should rule.

Hen nights

- The rules are that there are no rules. Be as brash, disgusting, perverted and menacing as possible…

- Just make sure the bride-to-be has a good time and isn't forced to do anything that will scar her or her intended for life.

- And try and keep hold of your knickers.

'All I want for Christmas...'

As soon as you hit 25 years of age, the season of goodwill becomes less about parties, presents and perhaps a snog under the mistletoe and more about stress, spending and salvation in a box of chocolates when you finally get some peace and quiet. How can you keep the Yuletide magic alive when you've found out about Santa Claus and you have to go back to work on 27th December?

Bah, humbug, to you, Ms Scrooge. Christmas is wonderful because:

1. You get lots of post.

2. You are forced to remember and send love to people you don't make time for during the rest of the year.

3. You can party every night if you want to.

4. It's the one time of the year hangovers at work are acceptable – almost mandatory.

5. You get to indulge your magpie fetish and cover your house in fairy lights and glitter.

6. When else can you have a supper consisting of pickled onions, after-dinner mints and smoked salmon, washed down with a pint of cream liqueur?

7. You receive presents – some of which you'll like.

8. You have to stay in all day with the fire on. You can't feel lazy because the gym is closed and no one else is at work.

9. You go home and act like a child again. You visit the local pub and bump into old school chums, get told off by your dad for scaring the cat when you stumble in

after midnight mass (the only time you make it to church all year) and your grandma runs around after you like you're a princess.

10. You play Christmas songs over and over and attempt to teach your teenage brother Ceroc. And he doesn't hate you for it.

Should we spend Christmas with our families?

Most children have a homing instinct when it comes to Christmas until they have children of their own. However, you can do your own thing. It could be less stressful to go away with your partner and friends – and often cheaper too – than to spend Christmas with your family. But it is important to remember your family's feelings, so perhaps...

♦ Hold a 'mini-Christmas' before or after to swap presents and catch up.

♦ Call in the morning to wish them well.

♦ Give them as much warning as possible.

♦ Don't show off about your modern, relaxed, stress-free Christmas. You mum's probably in the kitchen with her hand shoved up a turkey.

♦ If you had fun, suggest you go away with your family next year.

♦ Don't avoid them too many years on the trot. They'll get paranoid.

♦ Be considerate. Try to make it home if you have a lone sibling who will have to take the full force of the family if you disappear.

For many couples, dividing time between both sets of parents is the biggest problem at this time of year. When you're young, free and single, it's automatically assumed you will be travelling to your parents on Christmas Day. Then you meet someone and his parents think the same. Yikes! The mums start asking in September what you're doing, both nervous that the other mum will get the upper hand. The same often applies to the children of divorced parents. You can:

◆ Go to one set of parents for Christmas Day and one for Boxing Day and alternate each year.

◆ Not see either. Enjoy being with each other and 'do the tour' when you feel ready, on Boxing Day or New Year's Day perhaps.

◆ Split up – let him go to his parents while you go to yours. It's a shame, but it stops inter-parent jealousy and you'll feel comfortable and know what to expect. You don't want to waste a Christmas with strangers who do things differently. If you're in the same town, you can always meet up in the evening when the relatives have fallen asleep in front of the telly.

◆ See both sets of parents. I'm not recommending you partake in two turkeys, but do one lunch and one dinner. My husband and I find this is the best compromise: lunch is a big deal at my parents', so we go there until 5 p.m., when we move on to his parents' where drinking, games and drinking games are important.

◆ Invite everyone to yours – that way if they want to see you, they can. However, your house is probably smaller, you're not such an experienced cook and your families might not get on. Save this option till you've really got fed up with them.

Avoiding Yuletide fights

We love our families, but familiarity also breeds madness. By midday, every little dig or smirk will make you consider hanging yourself from the tree with a bit of tinsel. It's no laughing matter: more people request antidepressants or divorces at Christmas than at any other time of year. How can you avoid total nervous or relationship breakdown?

◆ Don't move in lock, stock and barrel for three days, just go for lunch.

◆ If something is worrying you, mention it in advance. Don't cause a scene as you're pulling the crackers.

◆ Respect your hosts' way of doing things. Even if you're at your parents', it's their home and if they want to play charades for three hours, they can do so.

◆ If you've got nothing useful to say, don't say anything.

◆ If an awkward situation arises, suggest a game or walk to defuse things.

◆ Don't overreact with embarrassment if you've bought along a friend or lover... Everyone knows families are bonkers.

◆ Try to see the funny side. You'll miss them when they're gone.

Who cooks?

The kitchen work normally falls to the hostess, or the women in the house. If you feel bad about this...

◆ Telephone in advance and ask what you can bring to help: a cheese board, the desserts...? You could even prepare and cook the vegetables so they only have to be microwaved minutes before eating.

♦ Too many cooks *can* spoil the broth, so if the hostess says she doesn't need any help, offer to serve drinks, lay the table or tidy up instead.

♦ If you require any special items (i.e. vegetarian nut roast), bring them with you to stop the chef stressing.

♦ If one or two people have done the bulk of the work, be thankful. Christmas dinners take a lot of preparation. Lots of 'yum' noises please.

♦ Whoever cooks should not have to wash up.

How much should you spend on presents?

It seems so long ago that gifts were simply tokens of love and thoughtfulness. In this advertising, style-conscious age we all seem so obsessed with how much things cost. We don't just want to receive the biggest boxes from under the tree, we want to give them too. But giving presents shouldn't be stressful if you follow these guidelines:

♦ Only spend what you can afford. No one would want you to get in debt on their behalf.

♦ Don't feel embarrassed to set a limit – it's better if you all agree to keep to a certain amount.

♦ Remember last year. What did each person buy you? What did you buy them? Did you feel stupidly tight or a bit extravagant? Pick their present accordingly this year.

♦ Try not to compete with the super-rich.

♦ Agree to have a no-present pact with some friends – you'll both be grateful.

♦ Spend roughly the same on siblings and parents to stop any comments.

♦ Some people – especially teenagers – genuinely prefer/ need money or gift vouchers. Don't get on your high horse and buy them something they'll never use 'because vouchers and cash are impersonal'.

♦ When it comes down to it, if you buy a present with care, attention and thought, it doesn't matter how much it costs.

♦ Keep all receipts and offer them to people after they've opened their presents – especially when buying clothes or jewellery.

♦ If you really hate a gift you've received but the person who gave you it really loves the gift you gave them, just thank God for your great taste and be happy you've made them happy. You don't give to receive.

JOANNE, 28

❛ I have a friend from my college days who has always bought me expensive Christmas presents. Most of my other friends and I either have a pact not to buy each other things or just to get token gifts and so I find it very frustrating trying to find a present in the price range I use with close family for a friend I have only seen for an hour's lunch in the entire previous year. It's terribly embarrassing if yet again my present looks pathetic next to hers. ❜

New Year's Eve nightmares

The night of new hope brings with it a lot of pressure to be sociable, fun and sozzled. But if you're not in the mood, rather than put a dampner on others' fun, admit defeat and stay in. Put your feet up with the Christmas leftovers. The television networks seem to store up the best programmes for the party night of the year – go figure – so chill. Or have a dinner party so you can drink champagne and celebrate in the comfort of your own home or persuade a friend (with a spare bedroom) to have a house party.

Admittedly, if you're single you want to be where the single people are and they probably won't be at any of the above. Sort out party tickets well beforehand (they sell out sharpish for NYE). Book a return taxi with a firm you trust, pay in advance if you can and tip well. You don't want your cabbie being tempted elsewhere. Eat and go to the loo before you go out – the queues and prices will shock the most regular of ravers.

Wherever you are, make midnight special – it really is lame to be tucked up in bed when Big Ben strikes (oh er). Or on your own. (NYE 1991: I was stuck in a nightclub toilet. Alone.) Link arms for 'Auld Lang Syne' (don't free-style in the centre of the circle) and mime the words as if you know what you're saying. Expect to kiss everyone within range – strangers too – but don't feel obliged to give them a full-on snog. If you're there with someone special – a close friend or partner – take a minute as near to midnight as possible to wish them well.

Happy Birthday?

Hooray! One year older, one year nearer to growing a moustache, losing your teeth and repeating the same old stories to any poor child that crosses your path. Policemen are looking younger and younger. You watch a rerun of *The Sound of Music* and find the Captain more alluring than Frederick, the eldest Von Trapp. And you've developed a penchant for goat's cheese. Everything that once was perky and polished is looking a bit grey and migrating south... and you're supposed to celebrate?

How old are you?

People need to know when people were born. As a journalist, I know no story is complete until we've uncovered an age to match a face – even if it's not the real one. I always say to my celebrity interviewees they can lie as long as I get a number. (They normally do lie.)

If you're asked your age and you don't want to answer, feel free to say 'Mind your own business.' Lying is tricky – there's always an old friend or family member to set the record straight. And I don't understand the need to lie anyway – you've earned that face! If you knock a few years off, people will think you look old for your age. And that's not good. You want them to say 'Wow, you look fantastic!'

Reminding everyone

In this busy world where modern girls have lots of friends and not a lot of time, birthdays can be forgotten. It's not malicious or intentional, just forgetful. So if you want to celebrate in style, you must take charge. Send out a circular e-mail to all buddies a month before the day, suggesting you all go out. Remind people why by saying you'll need to drown your sorrows at reaching the grand old age of XX. Try to steer clear of Friday or Saturday nights, when most people are busy with their partners or family. And don't suggest a weekend away solely in your honour – time off and hard cash are valuable to modern girls. Suggest a weekend away at the time of your birthday if you want, but don't make it feel like the sole reason for a break. And don't expect everyone to drop everything just because it's your birthday.

NB On the big numbers, someone might throw you a surprise party. Even if you suspect before the night in question, play dumb. That's half the fun for the guests. Feel free to cry or scream with surprise – in a moment of genuine delight like this, we can make the strangest of sounds. If you really don't like surprises, be gracious. Your friends have gone to a lot of effort and had your best intentions at heart. And the good thing is, for surprise parties, all kinds of people come out of the woodwork to make an appearance.

Working birthdays

Most people have to go to work on their birthday. If you work with a good team, e-mail everyone a few days before and suggest using your birthday to escape sandwich-at-the-desk syndrome and try out the new restaurant round the corner. Don't push anyone. Those who want to join you will reply within 24 hours. Some folks may not like socialising at work, so don't get paranoid it's a slight against you. If you're feeling flush, bring in birthday cakes for everyone to share with afternoon tea.

When it's someone else's birthday at the office, organise a whip round to buy them a bunch of flowers – a few quid per person should do it. Don't arse-lick the boss by buying a present on your own – get everyone involved.

If you can't bear the thought of working on your birthday, persuade your boyfriend, mum or best friend to take the day off too and go to the cinema or a spa.

Far and away

Forget money, it's holidays that make the world go around. After weeks of hard graft, grey offices and grey skies, it's great to escape to the sun, sand and sea. Or the countryside. Or the ski slopes. Basically, it's just great to get away. But whether or not you are gratefully received at the other end depends on how you behave as a tourist. If you're always respectful and considerate of the world's differences, you can't go far wrong. Or you'd think not...

Top tips for flying with style

Plane journeys are tiring and stressful and you tend to emerge the other end feeling like a bloated, greasy ogre. It takes a full day to recover, or longer if you're flying long-haul and there's jet lag involved. Here's how to minimise the damage:

1. Get rid of your cases as soon as possible and only carry on a small bag. Not only will it save your back, but also it's impolite to hog all the overhead compartments and you won't hold up people trying to get past you while you're rearranging your things.

2. Pre-book or request an aisle seat so you can stretch your legs and take trips to the loo without disturbing the sleeper at your side.

3. Only recline your seat after meal times and take-off.

4. Don't wear restrictive clothing like jeans and shirts which make you sweaty during the journey. Do a Joan Collins – look smart in the lounge then change into a tracksuit on board.

5. Lay off the booze and caffeine – no one likes a hyper-drunk in close proximity when they're flying. Instead, ask the 'trolley dollies' for water throughout the flight and have an orange juice to boost your vitamin C.

6. Don't get angry and shout at parents of screaming kids – they're already mortified. (Unless the kids are running around or kicking your seat. In that case, by all means have a word about their 'angels'.)

7. If you are sitting next to someone who is taking up too much space or listening to music too loudly, tell them as soon as it starts to annoy you. If the annoying trait cannot be personally addressed (i.e. they are pissed, smelly and/or spitting on your dinner), tell a sympathetic air steward. They will try and move you rather than make a scene. Whichever course of action you take, do not suffer in silence.

Love the differences

Stop moaning about prices, people or political persuasions. Appreciate every country on its own merits. Try to be a patriotic citizen of the world. Explore and learn. Respect the country you're visiting and you become a good advert for your own. Nothing is more vulgar than travelling lager louts smashing up bars, eating roast dinners, abusing locals… and then moaning about having a crap holiday.

Funny food

Don't ever be rude about another country's specialities. Asians think British people are smelly for consuming so much dairy produce, so who are we to judge? Just order with caution, stick to rice and vegetables if you can't understand, buy bottled water and avoid ice.

Dress with respect

When staying in a hotel or mixing with other guests, dress appropriately. Before your stay, check to see if men need to wear shirt and tie combos to dinner, or if women are allowed to lunch in their swimming gear or must get dressed. Always take a long-sleeved top, knee-length skirt and hat in case you decide to visit a religious site.

JULIA, 26

❝ Last year, I went on holiday to Pakistan. As a mark of respect for local traditions my travelling companions and I wore shalwar qameez – traditional loose-fitting shirt and trousers – and headscarves. Given the temperature (50 C in Peshawar), this was quite a punishment at times. Nevertheless, we battled the heat, covered from head to toe. In a remote village we stopped to wash our clothes. I slightly hitched up my trousers to avoid them getting wet and waded into the water. Across the river came the noise of children and women shouting. I looked up and the next thing I knew they were hurling rocks at me because I showed an ankle. After 20 days staying in dormitories, I insisted on staying in a four-star international hotel. I spent the day swimming – the only woman to do so. Mothers sat around the pool while their children swam with their fathers. I was, needless to say, stared at. It's strange to feel so rude for showing your body. But proves that it's sometimes easier to follow customs, even if you don't agree with them.

Talking the lingo

Making a little effort is all it takes... Before you travel, look up and learn the words for 'hello', 'goodbye', 'thank you' and 'cheers'. They'll get you a long way.

When abroad, the answer isn't to talk slowly and loudly in your own language. That's just rude. Get your hands on a phrasebook for difficult times and make it clear you appreciate others' efforts to understand you. If they speak English, be humble and gracious.

Secrets of Success

◆ Be a pin-up girl and get a bit 'double D' – dignity and decorum will get you through the most testing of times with your head held high.

◆ When you hear someone has died, send a note then let the grieving grieve in their own time. Don't offer to come and help them clear out the deceased's house or tell them to get over it.

◆ Funerals are not the time to discuss your new car or great promotion. Shut it.

◆ Caring for the bereaved doesn't finish with the funeral. Check up on them regularly until you are sure they are a little better. Let them guide you as to what they need.

◆ Don't stand up, laugh or clap at weddings or christenings unless the couple and/or minister seem OK with it.

◆ Never let your children run wild at any big event. You think they're cute because you love them. They're nuisances to everyone else.

◆ It's rude to leave just one person wearing a paper hat after Christmas lunch. Keep yours on to stop the spirited guest sobering up – or looking back at photos and feeling a fool.

◆ At Christmas keep a stock of 'male' and 'female' gifts in your car or handbag in case someone unexpectedly hands over a pressie.

◆ Use first-class stamps when posting your Christmas cards – second-class ones seem unnecessarily stingy.

◆ If your gran's bought – or even worse, knitted – you a festive jumper, wear it. It will make her happy and at least your friends can't see you.

◆ Joint birthday parties can be fun but joint weddings are never a good idea.

◆ When travelling, don't push to get on or off a plane. Nothing can happen without you. If someone is having trouble with their luggage, offer a helping hand. Keep everything you need for the flight (lip balm, water, magazines) in the seat pocket in front of you so you don't disturb your plane partner.

◆ When you arrive in a foreign country, make sure you have at least a little local currency, including, if possible, some small notes or coins for tips and cab fare. Try to get to grips with

local money as soon as you can – you'll look foolish and dis-
organised handing over large notes for an apple.

♦ Don't feel obliged to make small talk with other tourists.
You're on holiday to relax. Be polite, but turn down offers to
dine or drink if you don't want to. If you bump into someone
you know from home, the same applies. Have a drink if you
fancy it – you may be grateful of a little entertainment
towards the end of your holiday – or suggest meeting up to
show photos when you get home if you'd rather be left alone.

♦ Don't be forced into attending welcome meetings or going
on day trips.

♦ Take sarongs and flip-flops if you're staying in a hotel. This
way you can wander through reception without feeling fat or
nervous.

♦ Factor tipping into your holiday. Keep small change for waiters, bellboys and any hotel staff who help you out. If you're
staying for a few nights, you can tip in a lump sum at the end
of your trip – although you might want to wave a carrot to
ensure good service.

♦ Not everyone wants to hear your conversation. Keep it quiet
in public places.

♦ Don't bore everyone with your holiday stories or pictures.
Editing is everything – both pictorially and verbally. If it was
really amazing, just say 'Everyone should see it before they
die.' That will get the point across.

Chapter Ten

Handling the rude, crude and undesirable

WHY ISN'T EVERYONE AS POLITE as you? You go out of your way to make people feel comfortable, normal and appreciated and even some of your closest friends can't be bothered to thank you for a gift or return an invitation! So your blood boils and you fantasise about crossing them out of your address book and never seeing them again. Is that the best way to cope with the socially inept?

Getting the upper hand

Being a confident, well-adjusted modern girl, you greet everyone as your equal – until they do you wrong. Then you need to put them in their place. Not to be cruel – just to make sure they don't make anyone else feel the same way.

1. Act with decorum – this should make you content, even if these idiots are trying to make you feel bad about yourself.

2. Try not to cry, shake or run away. That'll be a small victory for the socially inept.

3. Don't retaliate. When someone butts in, takes the mickey, tells a bad joke or burps, they want people to react – that's where they get their strength from. Ignore them.

4. If a wrongdoing has occurred (injury, pushing in, etc.), stand up for yourself politely, quietly and diplomatically. Tell the person their behaviour has upset you.

5. If they still won't correct their behaviour, turn the tables on them. 'You're incredible! It must be great fun to be so offensive and impolite, but don't you ever feel guilty?' Keep the tone light, as if you are genuinely interested – and what can they say? Even if they ignore you, everyone within earshot will enjoy your bravery.

6. Fight fire with fire if needs be. If Ms Arrogant is getting your goat, show off twice as much as her (as long as anyone else within earshot knows what you're doing). If Mr Dull is refusing to make conversation, don't help him out: stare at him blankly until he plays ball.

NB When someone reallllyyyyyy annoys you – and you *know* they're in the wrong – take a breather and say to yourself, 'Thank God I'm not such a freak.' Walk away if you can. If you can't turn on your heel, gently reprimand their bad behaviour: 'You can't say things like that anymore, Uncle Racist. Did you read that piece in the newspaper yesterday? It actually proved that...' Back up your light tellings-off with facts and figures, so it doesn't seem as though it's just you who disagrees, but the whole free-thinking world. And have a bitch about them afterwards if it helps you get it off your chest.

Stupidity

There is a difference between bad manners and not knowing good manners. Use your brain. You can tell if someone is being spitefully impolite or simply doesn't know any better. If a child, close friend or family member makes a social error, correct them gently in private and offer to lend them this book. If you don't know the person too well, ignore it. No harm done. Just feel fortunate you know right from wrong.

Iris, 26

❝ A friend once loudly complained in a restaurant about her gazpacho soup being cold – she assumed it should have been served hot. As soon as she'd stopped barking at the waiter, we told her the score and still have a good laugh about it today. She wasn't making a major social *faux pas*, it was a tiny culinary error. ❞

Forgive and forget?

Every time someone close to you lets you down, your heart will break a little. Not in a romantic way, in a realisation way. You will become more cynical, less trusting and a little tougher.

So if someone lets you down seriously, should there be any going back? In a perfect world, we'd all forgive and forget, but each individual case deserves careful consideration. If a lifelong friend lets you down once, ask them why. Think about external factors: were other people putting them under pressure, were they stressed or depressed, did they know you'd take it this badly? If, deep down, you know it's worth the battle, get over the problem and agree to put the past behind you. It could make your relationship stronger.

Letting go

Sometimes, however, people change and discrepancies can't be made up. If someone is repeatedly letting you down or making you feel terrible, think about whether you want this person in your life. If the negatives outweigh the positive, don't put up with their crap. Every relationship needs give and take – just make sure it's not always the same person giving and the same person taking. Resentment is not a good foundation for a healthy friendship.

> **JANE, 24**
>
> ❝ I recently went away with my schoolfriends for the weekend. I took a few bottles of champers with me because I had an announcement to make: I was getting married. The girls took my bubbly, but wouldn't shut up so I could tell my news. In the end I told one of them and she kind of smirked and shouted it to the others, some of whom gave me a kiss while telling me I was too young. The next day we were supposed to meet at 10 a.m. to go swimming. They weren't at the meeting-place so I knocked on all their doors. They weren't there. Three hours later, they knocked for me, saying they hadn't been able to sleep and had gone for a walk along the beach together. I cried. It seems like a small thing, but I thought it was very selfish and disrespectful of them. Sadly, I haven't got many friends, so I probably won't rock the boat with them, although any social event with them now is a real strain as they continue to leave me out. ❞

Avoiding people

If you really can't stand someone, keep out of their way. Spending an hour in their presence will bring you out in a rash, and to be honest, they are probably not worth stressing over. If you know in your heart of hearts you've made the effort and behaved with kindness, you've got a clear conscience. Refuse invitations to events you know they'll attend. Spend less time with the friends who insist on admiring the loser. Meet new, interesting people through work or hobbies.

The hate brigade

Some people will hate you whatever you do. They've made up their mind and you can't change it. Well, don't worry... it's *their* problem. People are cruel to others for very few reasons – and it often doesn't have anything to do with whether or not the person deserves it.

1. Jealousy – the quickest way to knock someone off their perch is to take the mickey or make them question their self-esteem. It's classic psychology: if someone is pretty, remind them they have a large rear end; if someone is in a good relationship, remind them of their boyfriend's past girlfriends. It's as transparent as a stained-glass window... but still hurtful, I know.

2. Misery – happy people are generally so busy being, er, happy that they haven't got the time to be envious, bitchy or backstabbing. Miserable people have lots of time for these occupations. Offer these people a hand, but if they refuse it, there's little you can do. They need to help themselves first – and don't get sucked down with them. Negative people are so draining.

3. Sexual attraction – another one I learnt in the play-ground: boys only chase and pull the pigtails of the girls they fancy. Men continue this in adulthood. If a bloke spends a long time teasing you about a mistake at work, he thinks he's flirting.

How to react to the world's most difficult stereotypes

Oh, if only everyone were as polite, accommodating and kind as us modern girls. Unfortunately, we're all different. Things you find offensive may be completely acceptable to others and sometimes the biggest test of your own good manners is how you deal with others' lack of manners.

Show-offs

If you want to share your own tale of success in love, work or play with another, 'moderation' should be the etiquette watchword. No one likes someone who endlessly crows on about their good fortune. Deal with these people quickly or they will become monsters. If you are on the receiving end of a bore, initially congratulate them, but try to bring another person/subject into the conversation once they have had a reasonable time to bask. We all need to be praised for our achievements, but there are limits. We should also be sympathetic to those whose own lives may not be going so well.

Beautiful people

They do nothing for your self-esteem. You feel fat and ugly in their company. You feel so bad in fact, you are forced to turn bitchy and make comments about them being dumb. Prepare for a night with supermodels or the equivalent by getting your hair done, wearing an outfit you feel comfortable in and reading the complete works of Shakespeare. Also remember, truly beautiful people don't realise how beautiful they are so don't feel intimidated. And beauty is only skin deep, anyway.

Pushy religious folk

Yes, you've gotta have faith – and it is a wonderful thing if you're lucky enough to find it. But it cannot be got from a leaflet shoved through your door or from watching a TV show with a tyrannical male damning us all to hell if we don't buy his video immediately. People find comfort wherever they can. Live and let live. Advise scary religious people you encounter to do the same. Equally, though, have respect for them and don't insult their faith.

Bitter feminists

Women should be equal to men, that's a given. Most modern girls feel equal – or better off. We get better exam results, find employment quicker (although there's still the pay issue to be sorted out) and have more choices. We should be able to stay at home or go to work once we have children. We can drink beer, understand the offside rule *and* wear low-cut tops. But some old-style feminists don't like us having the best of both worlds. They've confined them-selves to a life of dungarees, mung beans and cats – and for what? Well, even if you can't relate to them, these women have helped forge the way, so be thankful and kind. And remember, not every woman over 40 with a cat is a lesbian.

OTT queens

Think of a gay man and what do you see? Abba, sequins and a few cool dance moves? Well, often yes. But there is also the gay man who isn't so keen to be a woman-friendly crowd-pleaser. In fact he finds girls repellent, thinks straight people are boring or has a wicked tongue that hurls insults indiscriminately. If you encounter such a King Charles spaniel, give as good as you get with humour – the only way to join his gang that doesn't involve a backstage pass to a Pet Shop Boys gig.

Walking groins

For these men, everything is an innuendo or a come-on. You can't head for the buffet without them making a comment about where they'd like to hide their sausage. If you run into a sad man like this, ignore him for as long as you can and he should get the hint. If he continues, warn him his remarks or offensive and sexist and you will make a complaint, or talk openly to all the other women in the room about his bad behaviour. They'll shake your hand for giving them a warning.

New mothers

Yes, you've had a baby, but so have lots of other women. You didn't invent childbirth. We don't want to hear about your dilated cervix or cracked nipples. Your kid might look cute but we don't want to discuss its belly button dropping off for two hours or watch you change its nappy. Please, modern girl, don't lose sight of yourself when you become a mum. Carry on watching the news, discussing sex with your mates and having the occasional alcoholic beverage. Raising a little person is the most serious job in the world, so give yourself a break when you're with your chums, ey? I thank God my mother-friends have stayed sane and can talk about things other than placenta.

Vain celebrities

Yes, they love themselves. Yes, they only talk about themselves. Yes, they very rarely carry cash. They go on all the time about being 'normal' and 'fat' when they are clearly barking mad and skinny. But who cares? Meeting a celebrity isn't an everyday occurrence and your encounter will give you a few tales for the pub. And you could sell your story to a tabloid for loads of cash. And no one takes celebs seriously anyway.

Mean and moody men

Grunt, grunt. They seem unable to conduct a proper chat. Everything's a drag. Every movement comes with a sigh. If they are handsome, the moodiness can add to their sexiness. If they're ugly, it just makes them even more disagreeable. Ignore the mean and moody if they're bringing you down – at least you know they'll sit down and not complain, just grumble to themselves. If you finally find yourself married to one, either tell him to buck his ideas up or enjoy the peace and quiet.

The windbreakers

Some people think it's funny to break wind, burp and make strange gurgling noises. My brothers, for example. But such an obvious display of bodily functions puts people off their food and makes them feel dirty. You can't be too sensitive, of course, – we all do these things (even the Queen and Madonna) – but if someone starts sharing a bit too much, ask them to stop. Say it makes you feels sick, and – the best way to get them to stop – say it makes you go off them.

> **EXCELLA, 28**
>
> ❝ People at my work – male and female – have no issue with burping and farting. There is no pretence of embarrassment. They are proud to burp loudly and obviously. They also leave floaters down the loo. We have crap toilets and we went through a stage of getting weekly, if not daily, e-mails about flushing your business away. How grim is that?! We now have signs in all the loos – even the 'client' one – stating: "Please leave the toilets how you would wish to find it." Yes – even the grammar is wrong. ❞

Family ties

Let's assume we all love and cherish our families… but on a day-to-day basis they annoy the hell out of us and vice versa. The problem with families is they know you too well. You can't escape the truth or try to become a smarter, sexier person (your dad will always be there with the naked toddler pictures).

When your family are getting too much, take a break. Make other plans. Keep in touch with letters, e-mails and postcards, but put the answering machine on when you get in from work so you can avoid your mother's nagging calls. Don't feel forced into attending dull family events or visiting them every weekend. Invite them to your home if it makes them more respectful. We can choose our friends but we can't choose our family. But we *can* choose whether they annoy us or not.

The out-laws

Just when you've got to an 'adult' relationship state with your own family, you get married and have a set of in-laws to deal with. This is tricky because there's no natural bond, you don't understand them and their loyalty will always be to your beau. Don't push things. Don't force yourself on them. Let your partner care for that side of 'the family', while you maintain yours (Christmas, birthday cards, etc.). You love their son/brother, not them, so don't worry if you don't see eye to eye. Just keep things civil and friendly for your husband's sake. More marriages break up due to family pressure and interference than infidelity, so don't make your man piggy in the middle. And remember, if his family raised such a great guy, they can't be all bad.

Complaining

No one should have to put up with poor service or bad quality goods, but it can be embarrassing to complain in public. If you don't know how to do it properly, that is. The most important thing is to make sure you're complaint is justified. If you are drunk, don't make a scene – perhaps write a letter citing your case the next day when you've sobered up. If you are with others, ask their opinion before you demand the sacking of the wine waiter. Be fair, be calm, be quiet.

1. Think about what you're going to say before you open your mouth.

2. Start politely – always give people the chance to apologise.

3. Avoid getting personal – you'll only weaken your argument. Stick to the matter in hand. Rude comments are unacceptable.

4. Think about what compensation you want. What will make up for your cold dinner or terrible flight? Suggest peacemaking options: vouchers, free drinks, a letter from the manager, etc. Then negotiate. Be reasonable but don't accept anything derisory or it will niggle you indefinitely.

5. When writing a letter of complaint or making a phone call, go to the top. Ask the receptionist or administrator for the complaints manager's exact name and title. And don't hassle for results – allow at least 28 days for a response.

When you are the rude one

If a polite person is rude one day it can upset them for weeks. They wake up with that 'left-the-gas-on' fear they are not a nice person and that they've let the side down. So how does a well-mannered, modern girl cope with such a scenario? Facing the problem head on is the best way…

Getting back on track…

♦ Think about what you said/did. Is there some truth in it? Do you feel guilty because someone is hurting but still feel that you needed to say your piece? If so, loosen up a little. You're fine – you acted with good intent even if everyone else is moaning.

♦ Apologise. It takes two to tango, but if you're losing sleep, be the first to say sorry. You're not backing down. In fact, you're acting with great dignity and maturity.

♦ Get over it. Guilt is an exhausting emotion. You haven't murdered anyone (I hope). The older we get, the easier it is to understand that all adults make mistakes.

♦ Learn from it. You're not as tough and cold-hearted as you thought you were. You don't like being cruel (even if it is to be kind). Adapt your future behaviour accordingly. Remember, having difficult times helps us understand other people's difficult times. Even horrible experiences teach us about people and how we interact.

> **NB Avoid people who make you feel sad**, angry, anxious, inferior or resentful. All these vibes are too negative to drag a modern girl like you down. Treat people the way you would like to be treated, and love your family and friends as honestly and generously as you can.

Being rude on purpose

Sometimes you're tired, irritable and can't be bothered to chat to people who bore you senseless and smell like cheese. You'd rather be in bed, the bath – or God forbid – purgatory than spend another minute making small talk. Here's how to get rid of them quickly:

1. Stare off into the distance when they talk and constantly ask them to repeat themselves when they finish a sentence.

2. If you meet a policeman, call him Plod to his face. If you meet a model, force-feed her chocolate. If you meet a politician, cry hysterically about what their party has done to your country. If you meet a teacher, moan about their short hours and long holidays.

3. Scratch yourself. And look like you're enjoying it.

4. Ask your companion if they've always been big-boned.

5. Ask your companion if they've always been male/female.

6. Flirt with their partner.

7. Shout. And laugh like a drain.

8. Eat from people's plates without asking, lick your fingers and delve back in.

9. Pretend you are a neo-Nazi, a stockbroker, an Islamic Fundamentalist or a computer analyst.

10. Ask for someone's phone number in the first two minutes, insist you have a lot in common and invite yourself round for Christmas. They'll move like lightning.

Minging tone

Some people – deliberately or innocently – speak with a sarcastic tone or a voice that can be misinterpreted by sensitive people. It is something to watch out for. Friends may get used to it, but a new boss or mother-in-law might not take the time and will have you pinned down as a sarky madam. The best guide is to just speak when you've got something pleasant to say, don't speak in a deadpan voice and don't try and be intelligently humorous around strangers. Sarcasm is the lowest form of wit, but the highest form of intelligence, and while academics may enjoy your perkiness, dullards will be insulted.

Saying the wrong thing

We've all done it – put our foot in it, and then opened our mouth a bit wider to get the other one in. The best thing to do is just apologise. 'That came out all wrong, I was nervous, do forgive me.' That's OK. 'That came out all wrong, what I meant was not that you're a big bird, just that you're big-boned... like me... see, I'm a right porker.' That's not.

If you've dug yourself into a hole and wish the ground really would just close over your head and swallow you up, walk away or keep quiet for the next ten minutes. Don't dwell on it and don't bring it up again, unless you feel it could poison your entire relationship. I said something silly to my husband's friend once about being late – and have regretted it ever since. I should probably have taken her to one side and told her it was a mistake before things got out of hand.

MEL, 32

❝ A freelance journalist I have worked with for a couple of years came into the office a little while ago and I said, "Oh, is it raining outside?" She looked a bit bemused and said, 'No.' I suddenly realised she actually had really greasy hair and that it wasn't wet outside at all. It was as bad as asking a plump woman to have a seat on the train because of her "pregnancy". Fortunately I haven't actually done this – amazingly, considering my track record of etiquette mishaps. ❞

Dumping a boyfriend

Nothing is as undesirable as a man who won't take the hint. And you're expected to have sex with him. Bleurgh!

Chucking a former loved one could be the one example when honesty is not the best policy. Don't list a number of repellent characteristics that make you nauseous. Instead, put the emphasis on yourself. 'I'm not ready' is a good one. As is, 'I can't give you what you need and it's making me feel worried'. Blame it on being immature/unfaithful/unsure/selfish – even if he's a vile, self-centred prick, your sole aim is to get rid of him as easily as possible. And to do so with as much decorum as possible. Do it in private, face-to-face and without hesitation. Don't go back on your word when he starts wailing.

Secrets of Success

◆ Non-RSVPers should be shot. They don't understand how 'keeping things open' sounds (like they're waiting for a better offer, basically). If you can't or don't want to attend, tell the host asap.

◆ Behave yourself in confined spaces. Cover your mouth when you cough, yawn or burp, fart on your own (even silent ones can be deadly for your social standing), keep tissues on you if you have a cold and wash on a daily basis (or more if necessary). Scratching is also a no-no.

◆ Don't discuss your trip to the loo. People don't want to know. Likewise if anyone tries to discuss their number twos, ask if they're worried about a medical problem you can give advice on. If not, tell them to zip it.

◆ Peeing in the street isn't a good idea. If you are caught short, try and find some grass to settle on – it's absorbent and the smell won't linger.

◆ Learn some diplomatic skills. Be tactful with people.

◆ Honesty is normally the best policy – for your own sanity, if nothing else. Telling lies or covering up can cause a lot of internal anguish. But if no one will benefit from a spoonful of truth juice, keep a lid on it.

◆ Teenagers are difficult to like: they're greasy, spotty, mono-syllabic and think you're uncool. Avoid them at all costs. You'll feel better and younger for it.

◆ If you are massively overweight and planning to travel, advise the company you're booking your tickets with. Some airlines are going to make the wide-loads buy two tickets in the future and they could have a point. Everyone should look how they want to... until they squash and injure their neighbour.

◆ Shop assistants who gossip with their mates while you're waiting to be served are the most evil people on Earth. Not only because they keep you waiting and refuse to make eye contact, but also because they bring out a violent streak you never knew was there.

◆ Snobby shop assistants are also foul. The customer is always right. Do they want our money or what?

◆ Bar staff that only serve members of the opposite sex are annoying, but hey, I suppose singletons have to get their kicks where they can. If you've been overlooked three times, draw the person's attention to it and try to get them on side. Waving banknotes rarely works, you'll just look a bit flash.

◆ Another evil of modern society is very thin girls who are always on diets. Why? If I looked like a lollipop, I'd move into a pizza parlour and get taken shopping in a wheelbarrow. Try to be kind when thin girls moan about being fat – we all have our hang-ups and they are not being rude about you – even if you are six sizes bigger. People only judge their own figures with such intense scrutiny but think of others as looking perfectly fine.

◆ If a friend won't forgive you an indiscretion, move on. Everyone has different boundaries of acceptability and if you've tried to be fair, it's their loss, not yours.

◆ When it comes to friends and acquaintances, it's quality not quantity that counts. Don't put up with the rude, crude or undesirable just to have another number in your mobile.

Further reading

Burrell, Paul, *Entertaining with Style*. André Deutsch Ltd, 1999.

Debrett's Correct Form. Headline, 2002.

McInerney, Jay, *Bacchus and Me: Adventures in the Wine Cellar*. Vintage Books, 2000.

Mole, John, *Mind Your Manners*. Nicholas Brealey Publishing Ltd, 2003.

Morgan, John, *"The Times" Book of Modern Manners: A Guide Through the Minefield of Contemporary Etiquette*. Times Books, 2000.

RoAne, Susan, *How to Work a Room: The Ultimate Guide to Savvy Socializing in Person and Online*. Robson Books, 2001.

Visser, Margaret, *The Rituals of Dinner: The Origins, Evolution, Eccentricities and the Meaning of Table Manners*. Penguin Books, 1992.

Index